I've GOT To Have That Recipe!

Barbara Doell,
Dianne Winsby
and
Pat Pollard

1987
Doubleday Canada Limited, Toronto, Ontario

Cover and food photographs: Ray Webber
Printed and bound in Canada by Friesen Printers
ISBN 0-385-25142-4

Canadian Cataloguing in Publication Data

Main entry under title:

I've got to have that recipe!

Includes index.
ISBN 0-385-25142-4

1. Cookery.   I. Doell, Barbara.   II. Winsby,
Dianne.   III. Pollard, Pat.

TX715.183 1987   641.5   C87-094081-3

The authors would like to thank all the friends, grannies, and aunts who shared their treasured recipes. All the ideas in this book have been handed down through families, taken from dusty string-tied shoeboxes in attics, from joint experimental creations, or from simply imploring friends, relatives, and chefs all with: "I've *got* to have that recipe!"

The authors would particularly like to thank Byron Johnson of Friesen Printers for his support, and Ray Webber for his artistic photography.

Cover photo: Classy Cheesy Chicken and Mushroom Casserole

To all those friends and relatives who endured unending ingredient and recipe conversations while we were writing this book—gather your strength, the next book is on the way!

INTRODUCTION

You've got to be kidding — another cook book! Next thing you'll come out with another high-flex low-bounce aerobics class, another Beta ray tanning studio, or heaven help us, another technique to effectively parent. If you took all the Cookbooks on display in any of our local bookstores, stretched them end to end in a row heading west, you could walk to the Kona coast without having a drop of sea water on your Fila thongs, not to mention papering the Empress Hotel inside and out with just the dustjackets. So if we need another cookbook we surely need another one size fits all jumpsuit, another tennis racquet made of out some recently described trace element, or another "no-cal" drink made with enough basic chemistry to create a neutron bomb.

Hold it — these women aren't nuts, they are not running from the men in the white jackets with the big nets — they created a first class wholesale dessert business — "NATHAN'S Original Cheesecakes" — out of ten pounds of sugar and a dozen pre-stamped cartons — so maybe they've just got something. Nathan's Cheesecakes originators even after the business was sold, would be flagged down on desolate stretches of the Coquihalla Highway and asked how to blend the topping of the Chocolate Kahlua Cheesecake; a bakery business so naive in its inception, yet so successful in its product and performance, that market analysts are still asking the question "What went right?"

Why not a cookbook, built on the same naive enthusiasm for good food and sincere concepts of great cooking.

What they have done is create a cookbook, by people who love to cook, love results, love genuine ingredients — but who don't care to spend half of Friday, and all day Saturday working on some sort of "Delight" that tastes remarkably like "Dreamwhip" with a tablespoon of Tia Maria or have a weekend work party to create a dinner for four using eleven pots, six bowls and some obscure ingredient, used once in a lifetime and only available in a kitchen suppy store that couldn't be found by an explorer scout using a contour map and a magnetic compass.

This is a book for people who love to cook, but who also love to do a whole lot of other things — many of these things on a day when they are expecting six new friends at seven for cocktails and a buffet.

This is a book in which everything tastes good, no surprises, no special items. This is not a book that conjures up the lost flavours of Tasmania, by using ingredients only available below the Tropic of Capricorn — in the spring, and tasting somewhat like the floor of a tent.

Everything is an old favourite, loved by many, revered by families and friends. Many of these recipes are great for kids, good both summer and winter, they are simple to prepare and cook, they are presented by people who love food, for people who love to eat and hang out in the kitchen, and best of all, are easy and the results are great.

Contents

Great Beginnings

Verlyn's Salted Almonds

These are great served with drinks and we like to make them for our friends at Christmas.

2-3 lbs. blanched almonds
olive oil
peanut oil
salt

In a dutch oven combine equal amounts of olive and peanut oil to a depth of 1 inch. Heat at medium temperature until oil begins to sing but not smoke. Cook 1 cup of nuts at a time, stirring gently until golden. Watch carefully. Remove from oil with a slotted spoon onto thick brown paper, sprinkle with salt and shake to coat. Continue with rest of nuts.
Cool thoroughly and store in jars in refrigerator.

This is a very old recipe and well worth the effort.

Eileen Rose's Antipasto

Another antipasto recipe! We truly believe this is the best.

¼ cup oil
3 green peppers, diced
1 - 2 oz. jar of pimento, diced
3 cloves garlic, minced
1 - 7½ oz. can of white flaked tuna, drained
1 - 14 oz. can sliced mushrooms, drained and chopped
12 ripe black olives, sliced
12 green olives, sliced
1 cup sweet mixed pickles, diced
1 - 10 oz. bottle ketchup
1 - 10 oz. bottle chili sauce
pinch of cinnamon
1 tsp. bay laurel, crushed
½ cup white vinegar

Put oil in large frying pan. Sauté chopped green pepper, garlic and

pimento in the oil until tender. Add remaining ingredients, bring to boil and simmer for 10 minutes.

Bottle ripen in refrigerator for at least 10 days. Serve with crackers.

This recipe can easily be doubled or tripled.

Molded Avocado Starter

Yummy!

1½ envelopes unflavoured gelatin
¼ cup cold water
2-3 large avocados
3 tbsp. lime juice
1 clove garlic, minced
1 small onion, finely chopped
⅛ tsp. red pepper flakes
1 tsp. salt
⅛ tsp. pepper
2 tsp. jalapeno peppers, chopped
¼ cup fresh parsley, chopped
½ cup mayonnaise
1 cup sour cream

In a saucepan, sprinkle gelatin over cold water and allow to soften for 5 minutes. Heat slowly until gelatin dissolves.

In blender, mash avocados. Add remaining ingredients, except the sour cream and blend well. Gently mix in sour cream. Taste for seasonings.

Pour into a 5 cup oiled mold and refrigerate for at least 4 hours. Unmold and serve with corn chips.

 # Nippy Cheese
in a Crock

Serve with Anne's Nova Scotia Oat Cakes (p. 75)

16 oz. Schneider's nippy cheddar cheese, softened
¼ lb. butter, softened
3 tbsp. rum
1 bunch green onions, chopped

Mix all ingredients together until smooth. Store in crock in refrigerator for 2 days before serving.

This keeps indefinitely and improves with age.

Chicken Nuggets

We hope your local drive-in doesn't hear about these!

3 whole boneless chicken breasts, skinned
1 cup (24) soda cracker crumbs
½ cup parmesan cheese
⅓ cup walnuts, finely chopped
1 tsp. thyme
½ tsp. tarragon
½ tsp. salt
1 tsp. garlic powder
½ cup butter, melted

Cut chicken into 1 inch cubes. In a small bowl, combine crumbs, cheese, walnuts, herbs & spices.

Dip chicken into melted butter and roll in crumb mixture.

Arrange nuggets on a foil-lined cookie sheet.

Cover and refrigerate or freeze. No need to thaw before baking.

Bake uncovered at 400°F for 15-20 minutes, or until golden brown.

Serve hot.

Makes 6 dozen appetizers.

Teriyaki Chicken Wings

These are wonderful!

2 lbs. chicken wings
2-3 tsp. sugar
¾ cup soy sauce
2 tsp. fresh ginger, grated
1 clove garlic, minced
¼ tsp. pepper
½ tsp. paprika
½ tsp. chili powder

Cut wings at joint and discard tips. Place wings on baking sheet, sprinkle with the sugar and allow to sit at room temperature for 20 minutes.

In a small bowl, combine rest of ingredients. Pour this mixture over wings and let sit for at least 30 minutes. Turn to coat occasionally.

Bake at 350°F for 40 minutes. Baste partway through cooking.

Try this for a light dinner with a salad.

Bacon-Wrapped Water Chestnuts

Simple and Easy!

1 - 5 oz. can whole water chestnuts, drained
¼ cup soy sauce
8 strips of bacon
¼ cup sugar

Marinate water chestnuts in soy sauce for 60 minutes or longer. Cut bacon strips in half. Roll each chestnut in sugar, wrap with a bacon strip and secure with a toothpick.

Place on broiler rack (to catch drippings) and bake uncovered at 400°F for 20 minutes, or until bacon is crisp. Turn once while baking. Drain on paper towels.

Serve hot.

Makes 16.

Sticky Chicken Wings

These are finger licking good — literally!

3 lbs. chicken wings
3 eggs, beaten
1 cup cornstarch
vegetable oil for frying
¼ cup soy sauce
½ cup vinegar
½ cup sugar
3 tbsp. ketchup
1 tsp. salt
½ cup red currant jelly
2 tbsp. lemon juice

Cut wings at joint, discard tips. Roll wings in beaten eggs and then cornstarch. Fry in a small amount of oil until golden brown. Remove wings with a slotted spoon and place on a shallow cookie sheet.

Combine rest of ingredients in a small saucepan and heat to boiling, stirring occasionally. Reduce heat and simmer for 10 minutes. Pour over chicken wings.

Bake at 350°F for 30 minutes, or until well glazed.

Make early in the day and reheat to serve.

Sesame Chicken Strips with Plum Sauce

Make these early in the day and reheat in oven when ready to serve. See picture opposite page 16.

2 eggs
2 tbsp. dry white wine
2 tbsp. lemon peel, grated
2 tbsp. sugar
2 tbsp. fresh ginger, grated
2 tsp. salt

2 tsp. garlic, minced
2 lbs. chicken breasts, skinned and boned,
    cut into 1 × 2 inch strips
vegetable oil for deep frying
10 tbsp. cornstarch
1 cup sesame seeds

Blend eggs, wine, lemon peel, sugar, ginger, salt and garlic in a shallow bowl. Add chicken strips and turn to coat thoroughly. Let stand at room temperature for at least 30 minutes.

Heat oil to 400°F.

Stir cornstarch into chicken mixture. Coat each piece with sesame seeds. Fry in oil in batches until golden brown (about 2 minutes). Drain on paper towels.

Serve hot with plum sauce (p. 151).

Makes 24 strips.

Hot Crab Fondue for Dipping

A friendly way to start an informal dinner while gathered around the table.

1 clove garlic, minced
1 can chicken broth
½ cup dry white wine
½ cup Swiss cheese, shredded
2 tbsp. flour
1 tsp. Worcestershire sauce
1 - 7½ oz. can of crab (or fresh)

Combine garlic, broth and wine in a saucepan. Heat to boiling and then reduce heat.

Combine cheese and flour and then add to broth/wine mixture. Whisk until smooth. Stir in Worcestershire sauce and crab. Heat until hot and serve with cubed French bread.

Wine Steamed Clams with Tomato, Garlic Sauce

If you like clams, you'll love these!
Make sure you have a fresh hot loaf of French bread for dipping.

Tomato Sauce

2-3 tbsp. butter
2-3 garlic cloves, minced
1 medium onion, chopped
3 green onions, chopped
1 - 28 oz. can Italian plum tomatoes
1 bay leaf
salt to taste
freshly ground pepper to taste

Clams

2 lbs. fresh clams in shells
2 tbsp. butter
2-3 garlic cloves, minced
1 medium onion, chopped
2 cups dry white wine

Parmesan cheese
Parsley

Tomato Sauce:
   Sauté garlic and onion in butter. Add tomatoes, bay leaf, salt and pepper and simmer for at least 1 hour or until thick, not runny. Adjust seasonings and remove bay leaf.

Clams:
   Wash clams under cold running water. In large Dutch oven, sauté garlic and onions in butter, add wine and bring to a boil. Add clams, cover and steam for 5 to 10 minutes or until shells open (discard the unopened clams). Spoon clams and wine sauce into large serving bowl, top with reduced tomato sauce and sprinkle with Parmesan. Garnish with fresh parsley.

Our Favourite
Crab Dip

This has become a Christmas Eve tradition served with "Bugles."

16 oz. cream cheese, softened
½ cup mayonnaise
1 - 7½ oz. can of crab (or fresh)
2 tbsp. chili sauce
2 tbsp. ketchup
1 tsp. lemon juice
½ tsp. Worcestershire sauce

Whip cream cheese and slowly add mayonnaise until well blended. Stir in rest of ingredients and mix well. Refrigerate.

This can be frozen for 2-3 months.

Hot Mushroom Dip

This can be made early in the day and reheated.

6 slices bacon, cooked and crumbled
1 small onion, finely chopped
2 tbsp. butter
¾ lb. fresh mushrooms, sliced
8 oz. cream cheese
½ cup sour cream

In a frying pan, cook onion and mushrooms in butter until tender. Add cream cheese and cook over medium-low heat stirring frequently until melted. (This should take about 5 minutes.) Turn off heat and stir in sour cream and bacon. Place in serving dish and serve immediately with crackers.

Makes 3 cups.

Pebe's Stuffed Mushrooms

20 large mushrooms
2 tbsp. butter
1 medium onion, finely chopped
¼ cup green pepper, finely chopped
1 clove garlic, minced
½ cup Ritz crackers, finely crushed
3 tbsp. Parmesan cheese
1 tbsp. parsley, snipped
½ tsp. seasoning salt
½ tsp. oregano, dried and crushed
freshly ground pepper to taste
⅓ cup chicken broth

Wipe mushrooms clean. Remove stems, chop and reserve.

Melt butter in large frying pan. Add onion, green pepper, garlic and mushroom stems. Cook until tender. Add cracker crumbs, cheese, parsley, seasoning salt, oregano and pepper. Mix well. Stir in chicken broth. Spoon this stuffing into the mushroom caps so that each cap is heaping. Place caps in a 9" × 13" glass baking dish with ¼ inch of water.

Bake uncovered at 325°F for 25 minutes.

Mushroom Strudel

This is better than delicious! We also use it as a vegetable dish.

2 tbsp. butter
1 lb. fresh mushrooms, sliced
3½ tbsp. flour
2 tbsp. butter
¾ cup milk
¾ cup whipping cream
1 tsp. salt
½ tsp. pepper
1 - 8 oz. package frozen puff pastry,
    thawed at room temperature
1 egg, beaten

Place mushrooms and 2 tbsp. butter in frying pan and cook at

Photo: Sesame Chicken Strips with Plum Sauce, page 12.

medium-high heat until mushroom liquid cooks away. Melt 2 tbsp. butter in medium saucepan. Whip in flour and cook 1-2 minutes. Add salt and pepper to taste. Add milk and cream all at once. Bring to a low boil, whisking constantly. Add the cooked mushrooms and bring back to a low boil. Pour this mixture into a bowl and refrigerate.

Roll out thawed puff pastry to a 12" × 16" rectangle. Cut this in half lengthwise. Place one half on a foil-lined cookie sheet. Spoon the mushroom mixture down the centre of this half of pastry leaving a ½ inch edge. Dampen edge of pastry and place second strip of pastry on top, pressing edges together with a fork. Score top of strudel and decorate with any remaining bits of pastry. Brush with beaten egg. Refrigerate 30 minutes. (If made early in the day, cover well and refrigerate.)

Bake at 375°F for 20 minutes, reduce heat to 350°F and bake 20 minutes longer.

Rest strudel before serving.

Scrumptious Scallops

Be sure to have a fresh loaf of French bread on hand to sop up this delicate sauce!

1 lb. scallops
1 shallot, finely chopped
salt and pepper to taste
½ cup Noilly Pratt dry vermouth
2 cups whipping cream

Parsley

Place scallops, shallots, salt and pepper in a saucepan with vermouth. Bring to a boil and simmer slowly for approximately 7 minutes. Remove scallops from saucepan with a slotted spoon and place in a bowl. Boil stock again and add whipping cream. Stir with whisk while bringing to a boil. Lower heat and reduce this mixture to about half. Put scallops back into thickened sauce and heat through. Serve immediately. Garnish with parsley.

Serves 4.

Curried Chicken Turnovers

Turnover Cream Cheese Pastry
> 8 oz. cream cheese, softened
> 1½ cups flour
> ½ cup butter (not margarine)
> 1 egg (well beaten for brushing pastry)

Curried Chicken Filling
> 1 cup chicken, cooked and finely chopped
> 1 cup mayonnaise
> ¾ cup Monterey Jack cheese, grated
> ⅓ cup almonds, finely chopped
> ¼ cup fresh parsley, snipped
> 2 shallots, finely chopped
> 2 tsp. curry powder
> 2 tsp. lemon juice
> ½ tsp. salt
> ¼ tsp. pepper

Cream Cheese Pastry

In large bowl of electric mixer, beat cream cheese, flour and butter until smooth. Shape dough into ball. Wrap and refrigerate about 1 hour.

Roll half of dough to ⅛ inch thickness. Cut into 3 inch circles. On one half of circle place about 1 tsp. of chicken mixture. Moisten edge of circle and fold dough over filling (half circle shape). Firmly press edges together with fork and prick top. Brush with beaten egg. Bake on ungreased baking sheet at 425°F for 12 to 14 minutes. Continue with rest of pastry.

Curried Chicken Filling

Combine all ingredients and refrigerate for 30 minutes.

Makes about 3½ dozen turnovers. Freezes well.

Soups

19

Cream of Artichoke Soup

Wonderful subtle flavour!

⅓ cup butter, melted and cooled
⅓ cup flour
2 - 14 oz. cans artichokes, water-packed and drained
3 egg yolks
3 cups half and half
1½ cans chicken broth
Salt & pepper to taste

Garnish: whipped cream
             chives, chopped

In a blender, combine all ingredients except salt and pepper. Blend until chunky. Pour into saucepan and whisk over low heat until thickened and bubbly. (Do not boil.) Season with salt and pepper. Top with a dollop of whipped cream and chopped chives.

Creamy Brie Soup

A blender soup for a special treat.

2 cups chicken broth
1 cup onion, minced and sautéed
1 cup brie, cubed
2 cups milk
½ cup chives, chopped

In a medium saucepan add broth, sautéed onions and brie. Cook and stir over medium heat until cheese is melted. Pour into food processor and blend until smooth. Return to saucepan, add milk and heat through. (Do not boil.)
Serve immediately topped with chives.

Serves 4.

20

Cream of Cauliflower Soup

The garnish of butter and nutmeg complete this elegant soup. See picture opposite page 32.

2 - 10 oz. cans chicken broth
1 large cauliflower, chopped
2-3 leeks, chopped, white part only
1 cup whipping cream
¼ tsp. nutmeg
salt and freshly ground pepper to taste

Garnish: butter
        nutmeg

In a Dutch oven, combine broth, leeks and cauliflower. Bring to a boil, cover and simmer for 15 minutes or until tender. Cool slightly.

In a blender, mix a portion at a time until smooth. Return to Dutch oven, add whipping cream and seasonings and heat to simmering. (Do not boil.) Serve immediately.

Garnish with a dollop of butter and a sprinkle of nutmeg.

Serves 4.

Doherty's Escargot and Mushroom Soup

Rave reviews for this one!

2 tbsp. butter
½ cup onion, diced
4 cups fresh mushrooms, sliced
4 - 10 oz. cans of chicken broth

6 tbsp. butter
¼ cup flour
2 cups whipping cream (or half and half)
salt and freshly ground pepper to taste

3 tbsp. butter
1 - 6 oz. can escargots (24-26), chopped
¼ cup fresh parsley, chopped
2 green onions, chopped
2 cloves garlic, minced
salt and freshly ground pepper to taste
¼-½ cup dry white wine

In a frying pan, melt the butter and sauté onions and mushrooms until tender.

In a large saucepan, add chicken broth, sautéed onions and mushrooms. Simmer ½ hour.

In a medium sized saucepan, melt butter over medium heat and stir in flour until well blended. Add whipping cream and whisk until thick. Season with salt and pepper.

Melt butter in original frying pan and add escargots, parsley, green onions and garlic. Sauté until tender.

Add all ingredients including wine to the chicken broth and heat through. Do not boil.

This can be made a day ahead and refrigerated.

Mulligatawny Soup

This is a hearty soup — a meal in itself. Serve with our graham bread (p.79) and your favourite cheese.

½ cup onion, chopped
1 carrot, diced
2 stalks celery, diced
¼ cup butter

1½ tbsp. flour
2-3 tsp. curry

3 - 10 oz. cans chicken broth
½ cup cooked rice
¼ cup tart apple, chopped
½ cup cooked chicken, chopped
¼ tsp. freshly ground pepper
⅛ tsp. thyme
½ cup half and half, heated

Sauté lightly first 4 ingredients. Stir in flour and curry and cook for 3 minutes. Pour in the broth and simmer for 30 minutes. Add remainder of ingredients except cream and simmer 15-20 minutes. Immediately before serving stir in hot half and half.

This soup can be puréed at this stage, but we prefer it chunky.

Zucchini Soup

What to do when friends bring you yet another zucchini from their garden!

2 lbs. unpeeled zucchini, chunked
1 large onion, chopped
3 tbsp. butter
2 cans chicken broth
1 tsp. lemon juice
¼ tsp. curry (or to taste)
salt and freshly ground pepper to taste

Sauté zucchini and onion in butter until tender. Put this mixture into blender and blend until almost puréed. Add rest of ingredients and heat to boiling point, stirring well with whisk. (Do not boil.) Serve immediately.

Salads and Dressings

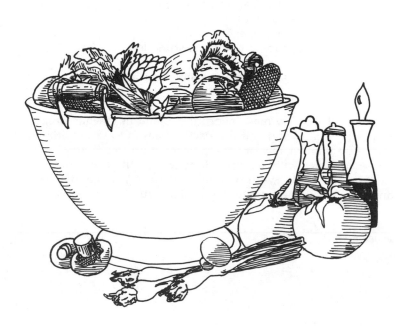

Bacon and
Avocado Salad

Hot and spicy!

¾ lb. bacon, cooked and crumbled
3 large ripe avocados
2 tbsp. vinegar
1 tsp. oregano
¼ tsp. ground cumin
2 cloves garlic, minced
1 can diced green chilies
cayenne to taste
salt to taste
4 cups iceberg lettuce, shredded

Garnish: 2 large tomatoes cut in wedges
tortilla chips

Peel, pit and coarsely mash avocados. Blend in vinegar, oregano, cumin, garlic, chilies and half the bacon. Season to taste with cayenne and salt. Use immediately or cover and chill up to 4 hours.

Line salad plates with shredded lettuce. Pile the avocado mixture in the centre and sprinkle with remaining bacon. Arrange tomato wedges around edge of avocado mixture. Garnish with tortilla chips.

Serves 6 to 8.

 # Cucumber Cream Cheese Mold

1 - 3 oz. pkg. lime flavoured gelatin
¾ cup boiling water
6 oz. cream cheese, softened
1 cup mayonnaise
1 tsp. horseradish
¼ tsp. salt
2 tbsp. lemon juice
¾ cup cucumber, peeled and grated
¼ cup green onions, finely chopped

Lettuce
Cherry tomatoes

Dissolve gelatin in boiling water. Add next 4 ingredients. Beat until smooth with electric beater. Add lemon juice and chill until partially set.

Peel and grate cucumber and drain on paper towel. Add onions and cucumber to gelatin mixture. Pour into oiled mold and chill. Unmold and serve on a bed of lettuce. Garnish with cherry tomatoes.

Dutch Boy Lettuce

Tangy, wilted lettuce salad with a hot bacon dressing.

4 slices bacon, cooked and crumbled
1 tbsp. bacon drippings
1 egg, slightly beaten
⅓ cup sour cream
¼ cup vinegar
2 tbsp. sugar
salt to taste
3 cups iceberg lettuce, shredded
6 cups spinach, torn
4 green onions, chopped

In frying pan combine egg, sour cream, vinegar, sugar, and salt and stir into reserved drippings. Cook and stir until thickened. Add hot dressing to spinach, lettuce, onion, and bacon, tossing until coated. Serve immediately.

Make Ahead Caesar Salad

Homemade croutons make the difference, and we've included our 2 favourite recipes.

Dressing:

1-2 large garlic cloves, minced
½ cup salad oil
¾ tsp. salt
¼ to ½ tsp. dry mustard
¼ tsp. freshly ground pepper
1½ tsp. worcestershire sauce
1 egg
2 tbsp. lemon juice

Salad:

6 slices bacon, cooked and crumbled
1 large head romaine
¼ cup Parmesan cheese
1 cup homemade croutons (see below)

Optional: crumbled blue cheese
6 chopped anchovies

Dressing: Combine all ingredients in a glass jar and shake well.
Salad: Wash and tear romaine into bite size pieces. Refrigerate until ready to serve.
When ready to serve: Toss greens, bacon, croutons and Parmesan with dressing.

Croutons for Caesar Salad

Method #1 — Garlic

1 cup fresh French bread, cubed
2 tbsp. oil
2 tbsp. butter
garlic powder, to taste

Cube enough french bread (without crusts) to make 1 cup.
Heat oil and butter in a frying pan and gently brown bread cubes on

all sides on low heat. Sprinkle with garlic powder. Cool. Enough for 1 salad.

Method #2 — Cheese
              1 loaf fresh French bread
              1 cup oil
              1 cup Parmesan cheese
              2-3 cloves garlic, minced

Cut 1 loaf french bread into bite size cubes (no crusts). Mix together oil, cheese and garlic. Toss cubes with oil mixture. Bake on cookie sheet at 350°F until browned. Watch carefully.

Makes enough for several salads and can be frozen.

Mushroom and Bacon Salad

A marinated mushroom salad.

              1 lb. fresh mushrooms, sliced
              3 green onions, sliced
              ⅔ cup oil
              4 tbsp. lemon juice
              1 tsp. Worcestershire sauce
              ½ tsp. salt
              ⅛ tsp. freshly ground pepper
              ½ tsp. dry mustard
              12 slices bacon
              lettuce

Slice mushrooms and put in a large bowl. Combine green onions, oil, lemon juice, Worcestershire, salt, pepper and mustard in a jar and shake until blended. Pour over mushrooms and mix to coat. Cover and refrigerate 4 hours or overnight. Toss occasionally.

Cook bacon until crisp and crumble. On each plate, lined with lettuce, spoon on the mushroom mixture. Sprinkle with bacon and serve.

 # Blender Green
Goddess Dressing

Also delicious as a sauce for fresh crab or shrimp.

1-2 cloves garlic, minced
3 anchovies, chopped
¼ cup green onions, finely chopped
¼ cup parsley, finely chopped
1 cup mayonnaise
1 tbsp. lemon juice
1 tbsp. tarragon vinegar
½ tsp. salt
½ tsp. freshly ground pepper
½ cup sour cream

Combine all ingredients in a blender, except sour cream and blend well. Fold in sour cream. Store in refrigerator.

Sharon's Honey and Garlic Salad Dressing

Our favourite for a green salad.

2-3 cloves garlic
1 heaping tbsp. liquid honey
1 heaping tbsp. Dijon mustard
1 heaping tbsp. mayonnaise
¼ cup vinegar
1 cup oil
salt and pepper (freshly ground) to taste

In blender mince the garlic. Add rest of ingredients except oil and blend well. Blend in oil slowly. Refrigerate.

We have varying tastes. For sweeter dressing add more honey, or for nippier dressing add more mustard.

Vegetables

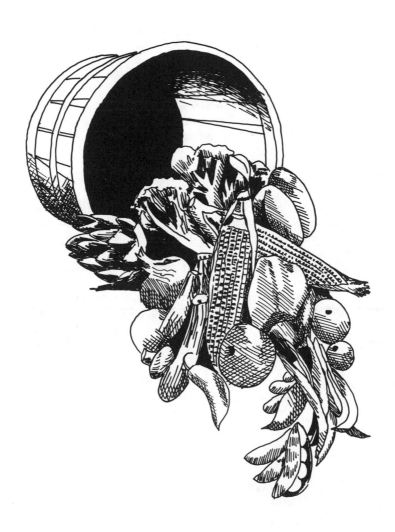

Auntie Honey's
Asparagus Continental

Excellent for a dinner party, and can be made ahead.

¼ cup butter
1½ cups fresh mushrooms, sliced
¼ cup flour
½ tsp. salt
1 cup asparagus juice, drained from asparagus
1 cup cream
3 egg yolks, slightly beaten
2 tbsp. pimento juice
¼ cup diced pimento
2 - 20 oz. cans asparagus cuttings, drained
1 cup buttered bread crumbs
½ cup cheddar cheese, grated

½ tsp. prepared mustard
3 egg whites

Sauté mushrooms in butter until tender. Stir in flour and salt. Slowly add asparagus juice and cream. Cook and stir until smooth and thick. Add egg yolks mixed with pimento juice. Remove from heat and add pimento and asparagus.

Mix the crumbs and cheese together, then alternate asparagus and crumb mixture in a 9" × 13" greased baking dish.

Beat egg whites until stiff and fold in the mustard. Spread over top.

If made ahead, refrigerate without meringue. Add meringue before baking.

Bake at 350°F, for 30 minutes.

Serves 8-10.

Photo: Cream of Cauliflower Soup, page 21.

Green Bean and Carrot Casserole

An easy company vegetable casserole.

6 large carrots, julienned
10 oz. pkg. frozen French style green beans
¾ tsp. salt
2 tbsp. butter
2 tbsp. flour
½ tsp. dry mustard
½ tsp. salt
⅛ tsp. pepper
1 cup milk
1 cup cheddar cheese, grated
½ cup fine dry bread crumbs
3 tbsp. butter, melted

Vegetables: Cook carrots in boiling water with ¾ tsp. salt for 5 minutes. Add green beans and continue cooking for 5 minutes or until vegetables are crunchy.

Sauce: In saucepan melt 2 tbsp. butter while vegetables are cooking. Sprinkle in flour, mustard, salt and pepper. Blend. Remove from heat. Add milk using a wire whisk to blend. Return to heat stirring constantly until boiling and thickened. Stir in cheese until it is melted.

Assemble: Butter a 9″ × 13″ glass dish and pour in drained vegetables. Pour sauce over vegetables. Combine bread crumbs with melted butter and sprinkle over casserole.

Bake at 350°F for 15-20 minutes or until bubbly.

Serves 8.

Green Bean and Mushroom Casserole

This can be made ahead and frozen. Nice with poultry, serves a crowd!

1-1 kg pkg. frozen French style green beans
1 can sliced water chestnuts, drained
1 lb. fresh mushrooms, sliced
⅓-½ cup butter
1 medium onion, chopped
2 cans cream of mushroom soup
1 oz. sherry
2 cups cheddar cheese, grated
dash worcestershire sauce
dash tabasco
freshly ground pepper to taste

¾ cup slivered almonds, toasted
1 cup cheddar cheese, grated

Cook beans for 5 minutes, drain and set aside.
Sauté mushrooms, onions and water chestnuts in butter until tender.
In large bowl, mix all ingredients except 1 cup cheese and almonds.
Pour into a greased 9" × 13" dish. Top with almonds and cheese and bake at 350°F for 30 minutes or until bubbly.

Serves 12 to 16.

Broccoli and Onion Casserole

Cream cheese sauce is what gives this casserole the great flavour.

> 1 lb. fresh broccoli
> 2 cups frozen whole onions
> or
> 2 cups fresh onions or leeks, chunked

White Sauce:

> 4 tbsp. butter
> 2 tbsp. flour
> ¼ tsp. salt
> dash of pepper
> 1 cup milk
> 3 oz. cream cheese

Topping:

> 1 cup sharp cheddar cheese, grated

Cut broccoli into bite size pieces and cook in boiling water for 3 minutes, drain.

Cook frozen onions according to package directions, drain. (Blanche fresh onions.)

Sauce: Melt butter over medium heat, add flour, salt, pepper and milk. Whisk until smooth. Reduce heat and blend in cream cheese until smooth.

Layer vegetables and sauce into a 2 quart casserole. Top with grated cheese.

Cover and bake at 350°F for 35 minutes.

Serves 8.

Linda's Orzo,
Barley and Mushrooms

Excellent as an accompaniment to chicken. Can be frozen and reheated.

2 cups (or more) fresh mushrooms, sliced
8 green onions, finely chopped
¼ cup butter
1 cup* orzo or long grain rice (preferably orzo)
1 cup pearl barley
2 - 10 oz. cans consommé
2 - 10 oz. cans water
salt and pepper to taste

Sauté mushrooms and onions in butter until tender. Add orzo and barley and stir until golden brown. Add rest of ingredients and cook on top of stove covered for 30 minutes (or in covered casserole in oven at 350°F for 1 hour or until liquid is absorbed). Toss and serve.

*Orzo can be purchased in the pasta section of your grocery store. Serves 8-10.

Skillet Peas with Lettuce
and Bacon

Tastes better than fresh peas from the garden.

6 slices bacon, cooked and crumbled
3 tbsp. butter, melted
1 small onion, finely chopped
2 - 10 oz. pkgs. frozen gourmet peas
1 cup iceberg lettuce, finely shredded
½ tsp. sugar
salt and pepper, to taste

In a large frying pan, melt butter and sauté onion until tender. Add

frozen peas and sugar and stir to combine. Cover and simmer until just tender (don't overcook). Add cooked bacon, lettuce, salt and pepper. Serve immediately.

Serves 8.

Bob's Spinach and Artichoke Casserole

2 - 14 oz. cans artichoke hearts, quartered
3 pkgs. frozen chopped spinach, drained and thawed
8 oz. cream cheese, softened
2 tbsp. mayonnaise
6 tbsp. milk
pepper
½-¾ cup Parmesan or Romano cheese, grated

Drain artichokes. Mix spinach and artichokes together. Blend together cream cheese, mayonnaise, milk and pepper. Stir cheese mixture into spinach mixture and pour into a buttered casserole. Sprinkle on enough grated cheese to cover top. Bake at 375°F for 35-40 minutes.

Serves 6-8.

Squash, Green
Pepper and Celery Casserole

1 - 10 oz. can cream of chicken soup
¼ cup milk
salt and pepper to taste
3 cups squash; any type, peeled and diced
½ cup celery, diced
1 green pepper, sliced
2 tbsp. butter

½ cup bread crumbs
3 tbsp. butter, melted

In a large bowl, blend together soup, milk, salt and pepper. Add vegetables and mix together. Pour into a buttered casserole. Dot with 2 tbsp. butter.

Mix bread crumbs with melted butter and sprinkle on top of squash. Bake at 350°F for 40-50 minutes or until tender.

Serves 6.

Bri's Mom's Squash and Orange Casserole

Squash dressed up for the holidays!

4 cups squash, any type, peeled and diced
⅔ cup brown sugar
2 tbsp. cornstarch
½ tsp. salt
2 tsp. orange rind
2 tsp. butter
1 cup orange juice, freshly squeezed

Place squash in a buttered casserole.
In a saucepan, mix next 6 ingredients together and cook over medium

heat until thickened. Pour over squash and bake at 350°F for 35-45 minutes or until tender.

Serves 6-8.

Apricot Glazed Sweet Potatoes

Excellent with turkey — a Christmas tradition.

>6 large sweet potatoes, peeled, chunked and boiled
>   until not quite tender
>¼ cup butter
>¼-½ cup brown sugar
>1 tbsp. cornstarch
>¼-½ cup water
>1 cup apricot jam
>1 tsp. orange rind, grated
>3 oranges
>½ cup pecan halves

In a saucepan melt butter, add sugar, cornstarch, water and apricot jam and heat on medium heat until slightly thickened. Grate 1 tsp. orange rind, then peel oranges and cut into thin slices. Add oranges, rind and pecans to butter mixture and heat through.

Place potatoes in a buttered casserole, pour orange mixture over and bake at 350°F for 15-20 minutes or until heated through.

Serves 6-8.

Crispy Tomato Layer Bake

Home-grown tomatoes seem to ripen all at once — here's a good way to use them. See picture opposite page 48.

4 slices brown bread, crusts on
4 tbsp. butter
2 heaping tbsp. parsley, chopped
1 garlic clove, minced
2 lbs. fresh tomatoes, sliced
1 cup cheddar cheese, grated
1 tsp. dry mustard
salt and pepper to taste

Crumb the bread in a food processor.

Heat butter in a frying pan, add crumbs, parsley and garlic. Fry gently for 10 minutes over low heat, turning continuously until brown.

Fill a buttered, ovenproof dish with alternate layers of tomatoes, crumbs, cheese and mustard. Sprinkle with salt and pepper between the layers ending with a layer of cheese.

Bake uncovered at 350°F for 30-40 minutes.

Serves 8.

Sunny's Zucchini and Carrot Casserole

Another Christmas favourite.

4 tbsp. butter
1 medium onion, chopped
10 medium carrots, peeled and chunked
10 small zucchini, unpeeled and chunked
1 can cream of chicken soup
½ cup plain yogurt
1 cup cheddar cheese, grated
¼ tsp. salt
¼ tsp. pepper
dash cayenne

1-2 cups seasoned packaged croutons

In a large frying pan, melt butter and add onions and carrots. Cook, stirring often, over medium heat until carrots are fairly tender (10-15 minutes). Remove from heat and cool slightly.

Meanwhile steam zucchini until crunchy. Drain.

In large bowl, mix together soup, yogurt, cheese and seasonings until well blended. Add zucchini and carrots, toss gently until well mixed. Place into a buttered casserole. Bake at 350°F for 15-20 minutes. Sprinkle croutons on top for last 10 minutes of baking.

Serves 10.

Zucchini Torta

5 eggs
½ cup onion, chopped
⅓ cup parsley, chopped
5 cups zucchini, grated and drained
1 cup Bisquick
¾ cup Parmesan cheese
1 clove garlic, minced
½ cup oil
1 tsp. marjoram
½ tsp. thyme
salt and pepper to taste

Top: ½ cup Parmesan
               paprika

In a large bowl, beat eggs. Add rest of ingredients, blend and pour into a 9" × 13" buttered casserole.

Sprinkle with ½ cup Parmesan and paprika for colour.

Bake at 350°F for 30-40 minutes, until golden brown and firm to touch.

To make ahead combine all ingredients except the Bisquick. When ready to bake, blend in Bisquick, pour into casserole, add toppings and bake.

Serves 10-12.

Main
Courses

Givetti — Greek Stew

This has a unique flavour. Don't be discouraged by the unusual ingredients or method; it is a crowd pleaser.

6 lbs. stewing beef
salt and pepper
½ lb. butter
4 lbs. onions, chopped
⅔ cup dry red wine
4 tbsp. red wine vinegar
2 - 6 oz. cans tomato paste
2 tbsp. brown sugar
2 cloves garlic, minced
2 cinnamon sticks
½ tsp. cloves
3 bay leaves
1 cup currants

Season stewing beef with salt and pepper. In a large Dutch oven, melt butter and add meat and mix well. Do not brown meat. Place the chopped onion on top of the meat.

In a bowl, mix together the tomato paste, wine, vinegar, sugar and garlic. Pour this mixture over the onions. Add cinnamon sticks, cloves, bay leaves and currants. Place a pottery plate* directly on top of the stew. Now place a lid on Dutch oven and simmer stew for about 3 hours. Do not stir. When cooked, drain off fat.

(*The purpose of the plate is to separate the fat from the stew.) Serve with rice or orzo (p.36).

Serves 10-12.

 # Judy's Marinated Flank Steak

1 large flank steak
1 large clove of garlic, minced
1 small onion, chopped
1 tsp. ginger, freshly grated
½ cup soy sauce
2 tbsp. brown sugar
2 tbsp. lemon juice
2 tbsp. salad oil
¼-½ tsp. coarse pepper

In a 9" × 13" baking dish, blend all ingredients except steak. Place steak in marinade and refrigerate for 8 hours or longer, turning once or twice.

Remove from marinade and barbecue or broil 3-5 minutes each side.

To serve, slice thinly on the diagonal.

This freezes well after being marinated.

We always triple this recipe, and freeze the extra two marinated steaks. When unexpected company arrives, dinner is in the freezer.

Serves 2 to 4.

Ted's Mom's Everyday Family Style Casserole

Kids love this!

8 oz. pkg. broad egg noodles
2 tbsp. butter
1½ lbs. ground beef
1 tsp. salt
¼ tsp. pepper
¼ tsp. garlic powder
1 - 8 oz. can tomato sauce
1 cup creamed cottage cheese
1 cup sour cream
6 green onions, chopped
1 cup sharp cheddar cheese, grated

Cook noodles, rinse in cold water and drain.

Melt butter in frying pan, add ground beef and cook until browned. Drain off fat. Add salt, pepper, garlic powder and tomato sauce. Simmer for 5 minutes.

In a large bowl, combine cottage cheese, sour cream, green onions and cooked noodles. In buttered casserole, alternate layers of noodle mixture with the meat mixture. Top with grated cheese.

Bake at 350°F for 30 minutes.

Serves 6 to 8.

# Baked Lasagna

We've made lots of lasagna — this is our favourite.

1 lb. ground beef
1 clove garlic, minced
1 tbsp. parsley, snipped
1 tbsp. basil
1½ tsp. salt
1 - 28 oz. can tomatoes
2 - 6 oz. cans tomato paste
2 strips (9" × 13" size) fresh lasagna noodles*
3 cups **creamed cottage cheese**
2 eggs, beaten
2 tsp. salt
½ tsp. pepper
2 tbsp. parsley, snipped
½ cup Parmesan, grated
1 lb. mozzarella cheese slices

Brown meat and drain. Add next 6 ingredients. Simmer uncovered for 30 minutes.

Combine cottage cheese, eggs, seasonings and Parmesan cheese.

Place 1 sheet of lasagna noodle in a buttered 9" × 13" glass dish. Spread ½ of the cottage cheese mixture over noodle and then cover with half the mozzarella cheese and half the meat sauce. Repeat the layers, ending with the meat sauce.

Bake at 375°F for 30 minutes. Let stand 15 minutes before cutting.

*If unable to purchase fresh pasta, use a 10 oz. pkg. lasagna noodles, cooking according to package directions.

Ted's Favourite Beef Stew

Adds a stroganoff flavour to stew!

6 slices bacon, cut into ½ inch pieces
2 lbs. stewing beef
2 cloves garlic, minced
2 onions, chopped
¼ tsp. marjoram
¼ tsp. thyme
3 cans beef bouillion
1 cup dry red wine
¼ cup ketchup
1 tbsp. brown sugar
1 tsp. Worcestershire sauce

1 cup sour cream
1 tsp. salt
pepper to taste

In a Dutch oven cook bacon pieces until just softened. Add stewing beef and cook until brown on all sides. Stir in garlic, onions, marjoram and thyme. Cook 5 minutes, stirring often. Pour in beef bouillion and bring to a boil. Stir in wine, ketchup, sugar and Worcestershire. Reduce heat and cook covered for approximately 2½ hours. Before serving, stir in sour cream and salt and pepper to taste.

Serve with buttered noodles and a crisp green salad made with honey and garlic dressing (p.30).

Veal Dijon

1 lb. veal strips, thinly sliced
2 tbsp. butter
salt and pepper to taste
½ lb. fresh mushrooms, thinly sliced
3 tbsp. shallots, finely chopped
¼ cup dry white wine
1 cup whipping cream
2 tbsp. imported Dijon mustard

Sauté veal strips in butter for about 1½ minutes. Season with salt and

Photo: Crispy Tomato Layer Bake, page 40.

pepper. Remove veal with slotted spoon and set aside.

Sauté mushrooms and shallots in same butter. Add wine and cook while stirring for about 3 minutes or until thickened. Add cream and cook 1 minute and then add mustard and cook 1 minute longer. Add veal strips and stir to heat through.

Serve immediately over hot buttered noodles.

Serves 4.

Veal with Avocado and Tomato

1½ lbs. veal cutlets (6 in all)
2 eggs, beaten
1 cup fine dry bread crumbs
2 tbsp. cooking oil
1 large avocado, cut into 6 wedges
1 large tomato, cut into 6 wedges
6 slices Swiss cheese

Have your butcher pound the veal very thinly. Dip veal into beaten eggs and then into bread crumbs.

In skillet, brown veal in hot oil about 5 minutes per side. Put veal into a 9" × 13" baking dish. Place one avocado and one tomato wedge on top of each piece of veal and cover with Swiss cheese.

Bake at 350°F for 5 to 7 minutes or until cheese is melted.

Serves 6.

Pork

Best "Barbecued" Spareribs

The title says it all!

Ribs

        4 lbs. pork ribs, back or side
        1 medium onion, quartered
        2 tsp. salt
        ¼ tsp. pepper

Sauce

        ¼ cup vinegar
        1 - 8 oz. can tomato sauce
        ¼ cup onion, chopped
        ¼ cup butter
        2 tbsp. Worcestershire sauce
        1½ tsp. salt
        ½ tsp. pepper
        3 tbsp. brown sugar
        3 tbsp. prepared mustard
        1 clove garlic, minced
        ½ cup water

Ribs: In 3 quarts water, place ribs, onion, salt and pepper. Bring to a boil. Reduce heat and simmer covered for one hour and 15 minutes (or until tender). Drain.

Sauce: In medium saucepan, combine all ingredients. Simmer uncovered for 25 minutes.

Arrange ribs in bottom of broiler pan without rack. Spoon half of sauce on top and broil 5 minutes. Turn, spoon over rest of sauce and broil 5 minutes longer.

Serve with baked potato and crisp green salad.

Bri's Favourite
Marinated Pork Tenderloin

Simple summer fare — good for barbecuing.

>2 pork tenderloins
>¼ cup soy sauce
>2 tbsp. chili sauce
>2 tbsp. liquid honey
>1 tbsp. oil
>1 tbsp. green onion, chopped
>1 tsp. curry
>2 cloves garlic, minced
>Tabasco and Worcestershire sauce to taste

Mix together all ingredients except meat. Place meat in sauce and marinate for at least 3 hours.
Barbecue for 5 minutes each side and cut on diagonal to serve.

Pork Tenderloin with
Rosemary and Sour Cream

>1½ pork tenderloin, cut into medallions
>1 tsp. rosemary
>salt and pepper to taste
>2 - 3 tbsp. butter
>1 cup sour cream
>2 cups sautéed mushrooms

Season pork medallions with rosemary, salt and pepper. Brown pork in butter until tender. Remove pork and set aside. Add sour cream and mushrooms to butter and stir to make sauce. Add pork medallions to sauce and heat through.

Serve with buttered noodles and a green salad.

Crispy Pork
Schnitzel With Dill Sauce

6 boneless pork loin cutlets, ½" thick
¼ cup flour
1 tsp. seasoning salt
¼ tsp. pepper
1 egg, beaten
2 tbsp. milk
¾ cup fine bread crumbs
1 tsp. paprika
3 tbsp. butter

Pound pork to ¼"-⅛" thickness. Cut small slits around edges to prevent curling. Mix together flour, seasoning salt and pepper and coat meat. Combine egg and milk and dip cutlets into egg mixture and then into a mixture of crumbs and paprika.

In large frying pan, melt butter and cook cutlets 3-5 minutes per side. Remove to warm platter.

Creamy Dill Sauce

¾ cup chicken broth
1 tbsp. flour
¼ tsp. dill weed
½ cup sour cream

Pour chicken broth into frying pan to loosen crusty drippings. Blend flour and dill weed into sour cream. Stir into the broth. Cook and stir until thickened. Do not boil. Pour over warm schnitzels.

Serves 4-6.

Butterflied Leg of Lamb — Dijon Marinade

Succulent! Make a day ahead.

>1 butterflied leg of lamb
>½ cup Dijon mustard
>2 tbsp. soy sauce
>1 tsp. rosemary or thyme
>1 tsp. fresh ginger, grated
>1 clove garlic, minced
>2 tbsp. oil

Mix together all ingredients in a blender, except lamb.
Coat lamb on both sides and marinate overnight.
Preheat oven to 450°F. Place lamb in a broiler pan in the oven and reduce heat to 350°F. Cook for 45 minutes for medium rare.
This can also be broiled or barbecued.

Greek Leg of Lamb

Saltspring Island, an island to the northeast of Victoria, is known for its splendid lamb. This is one of our favourite ways to cook a leg of lamb.

6-7 lb. leg of lamb
1½ tsp. salt
¼ tsp. pepper
3 cloves garlic (cut into thin slivers)
¼ cup butter, melted
¼ cup lemon juice
1 tsp. rosemary

Rub surface of lamb with salt and pepper. Cut 12 to 16 small slits about 1 inch deep into lamb. Insert garlic slivers into slits. Place lamb in shallow roasting pan and brush with melted butter. Pour lemon juice over meat and sprinkle with rosemary.

Roast at 325°F, uncovered for 2-2½ hours or until meat thermometer registers medium. Baste several times during cooking. Let roast stand for 20 minutes for easier carving.

Serves 8-10.

Classy Cheesy Chicken and Mushroom Casserole

See picture on cover.

8 chicken breast halves
½ cup flour
salt and pepper to taste
1 tsp. tarragon
¼ cup oil
¼ cup butter
2 cups sour cream
1 heaping tsp. tarragon
¾ lb. cheddar cheese, grated

1 lb. broccoli, cut into bite size pieces
2 cups cherry tomatoes
2 cups mushrooms, sliced

In a plastic bag, put flour, salt, pepper and tarragon. Add chicken breasts and shake until chicken is well coated.

Brown chicken in melted butter and oil in a skillet until skin is crisp. Remove chicken and put it in a baking dish. Pour off all but ¼ cup drippings.

Add sour cream to drippings in skillet and mix well. Pour mixture over chicken. Sprinkle with tarragon and cover with cheese.

Cook uncovered at 375°F for ¾ hour.

Add broccoli, cherry tomatoes, and mushrooms. Cover and cook 15-20 minutes longer.

Serves 6-8.

 # Wendy's Chicken Cacciatore

Serves 16-20. Make this 12 to 24 hours in advance.

>20 chicken half breasts and 10 thighs
>   or 4 cut-up chickens
>½ cup flour
>2 tsp. salt
>½ cup oil
>1 medium onion, chopped
>½ cup celery, chopped
>½ cup green pepper, chopped
>1 bottle chili sauce
>½ cup water
>1 tbsp. worcestershire sauce
>3 tbsp. brown sugar
>pepper to taste

Put chicken in plastic bag with flour and salt and shake well.
Heat oil in skillet and fry chicken until browned.
Drain chicken on paper towels and place in a large casserole.
Pour all but 2 tbsp. of oil from pan, add chopped onion and sauté until tender. Add rest of ingredients and simmer 10-15 minutes.
Pour sauce over chicken, cover and put in refrigerator for 12-24 hours.
Bake covered in 350°F oven for 2 hours. Watch carefully.

Crisp Baked Chicken

>1 - 2½-3 lb. fryer, cut up
>¾ cup sour cream
>2 tbsp. lemon juice
>1 tsp. rosemary
>¼ tsp. salt
>pepper to taste
>¼ cup corn flakes, crushed
>dash paprika
>1 tbsp. parsley, chopped

Arrange chicken in shallow baking dish. Combine sour cream, lemon juice, rosemary, salt and pepper. Spread half this mixture over chicken and bake uncovered for 50 minutes at 375°F. Cover with remaining sour

cream mixture and sprinkle with crumbs and paprika. Continue to bake for 10 minutes. Garnish with parsley.

Serves 4.

Bunty's Chicken Casserole

This is a good family or luncheon casserole as it uses leftover chicken or turkey.

2 cups celery, thinly sliced
   (or 1 cup celery and 1 cup water chestnuts)
1 onion, chopped
2½ cups fresh mushrooms, sliced
2-3 tbsp. butter
3 cups cooked chicken, cut into bite size pieces
1 can cream of mushroom soup
1 cup milk or half 'n' half
1 - 13 oz. can dried Chinese noodles
½ cup slivered almonds, toasted
salt, pepper, tabasco, paprika, dry mustard to taste

1 cup sharp cheddar cheese, shredded
1 cup potato chips, crushed

Sauté celery, onion and mushrooms in butter. Add rest of ingredients except cheese and potato chips. Mix well and place into a 2½ quart baking dish.
Top with cheese and potato chips.
Bake at 375°F for 40 minutes.

Serves 8.

Les' Chicken Divan

Outstanding! A nice luncheon dish.

6 chicken breast halves
1 can chicken broth
½ cup water
1 tsp. seasoning salt
fresh broccoli or asparagus to cover a 9" × 13" dish
1 can cream of mushroom soup
1 can cream of chicken soup
1 cup sour cream
¼ cup sherry
½ tsp. curry
pepper to taste
1 cup cheddar cheese, grated

Poach chicken in broth, water and salt for 20 minutes. Skin, debone and cut into ¼" slices.

Blanche broccoli and place in bottom of 9" × 13" glass dish and cover with chicken slices.

Mix rest of ingredients except cheese and pour sauce over chicken. Sprinkle with cheddar cheese and bake at 350°F for 45 minutes or until bubbly and heated through.

Serves 6-8.

Easy Chicken

A quick, casual family or company dinner. Serve with garlic bread and a salad.

1 - 10 oz. can cream of celery soup
½ cup dry white wine
seasoning salt to taste
ground pepper to taste
6 halved chicken breasts, skinned
6 slices swiss cheese
1 tbsp. butter
½ cup bread crumbs
2-3 tbsp. parmesan cheese
1 tsp. garlic powder
2 tbsp. melted butter

Combine soup, wine and seasonings in a bowl. Place chicken in

58

lightly greased casserole and cover with cheese slices. Pour sauce over chicken and dot with butter.

Top with a mixture of bread crumbs, parmesan cheese, garlic powder and melted butter.

Bake at 350°F for 50-60 minutes.

Serves 6.

Ham and Spinach Stuffing for Turkey

The ultimate stuffing!

1 lb. fresh mushrooms, sliced
1 cup onions, chopped
½ cup butter
2 - 8 oz. pkgs. herb seasoning stuffing mix
2 - 10 oz. pkgs. frozen, chopped spinach, thawed & well drained
3 cups cooked ham, finely chopped
15 oz. ricotta cheese
1 cup parmesan cheese
3 eggs, beaten
½ cup parsley, chopped
¼ tsp. salt
⅛ tsp. pepper

½ cup chicken broth

Cook mushrooms and onions in butter until tender.

In a large bowl place stuffing mix and add mushroom mixture and toss to coat. Squeeze spinach to remove water and stir into stuffing mixture.

Combine ham, cheeses, eggs, parsley, salt and pepper and add to stuffing mixture.

Use about 8 cups stuffing to stuff a 10-12 lb. turkey. The remaining stuffing can be blended with chicken broth and placed in a casserole. Cover and bake at 325°F for last hour of roasting.

This makes 15 cups of stuffing.

 # Lee's Chicken and Mushrooms

Quick and easy.

⅓ cup butter
½ tsp. rosemary
2 tsp. paprika
1 tsp. salt
¼ tsp. pepper
3 lbs. chicken, cut in pieces
¼ cup flour
½ cup dry white wine
3 cups fresh mushrooms, sliced

Preheat oven to 375°F. Put butter in a 9" × 13" baking dish and place in oven until butter melts. Remove from oven. Stir in spices.

Coat chicken in flour and place in the baking dish, turning chicken in butter-spice mixture until well coated.

Bake for 30 minutes uncovered, then top with mushrooms and add wine. Cover with foil and bake 30 minutes longer.

For a more elegant dish use boneless, chicken breasts.
Serves 4.

Dilly Baked Cod

1 lb. fresh or frozen cod fillets
⅓ cup plain yogurt
2 tsp. prepared mustard
2 tsp. onion, finely chopped
2 tsp. dill weed
1½ tbsp. mayonnaise
salt and pepper to taste
2 tbsp. parmesan cheese
½ cup cheddar cheese, grated
dash paprika

lemon wedges to garnish

Preheat oven to 450°F. Arrange cod in greased glass baking dish. In a small bowl combine yogurt, mustard, onion, dill weed and mayonnaise. Salt and pepper fish and spread yogurt mixture over fish. Bake 10-12 minutes per inch of thickness of fish.

Sprinkle fish with the cheeses and paprika. Broil for 1 minute. Serve with lemon wedges.

Serves 4.

Judy's Oyster, Chicken, Mushroom Stew

4 tbsp. butter
½ medium onion, minced
½ green pepper, finely chopped
1 lb. whole button fresh mushrooms
½ tsp. salt
⅛ tsp. black pepper

¾ cup whipping cream
1 cup milk
⅛ tsp. nutmeg
⅛ tsp. black pepper
¾ tsp. salt
4 tbsp. butter
4 tbsp. flour
2 tbsp. parmesan cheese

2 cups chicken, cubed
1 cup fresh oysters (washed and drained)
⅓ cup dry white wine (warmed)
½ cup fine, dry bread crumbs

Melt butter in skillet, add onion, green pepper and sauté over low heat until onion is tender. Add mushrooms, salt & pepper and sauté for 5 minutes. Set aside and keep warm.

Heat whipping cream, milk, nutmeg, pepper and salt in saucepan over medium heat. Blend flour and melted butter together and beat gradually with whisk into hot milk mixture until it thickens and is smooth. Add Parmesan cheese and stir until just melted and blended.

Add chicken, oysters (chopped or whole) to mushroom mixture. Add warmed wine and pour into a greased 9"×13" casserole. Sprinkle with bread crumbs. Bake at 450° for 20-25 minutes or until lightly browned and bubbling.

Serves 8-10.

Spinach Stuffed Salmon

Superb!

4-5 lb. whole salmon
salt and pepper

Stuffing:

10 oz. pkg. frozen, chopped spinach
6 strips of bacon, chopped
1 small onion, chopped
1 cup fresh mushrooms, finely chopped
1½ cups mozzarella cheese, grated
salt and pepper to taste
oil

Clean and debone salmon (leave skin on). Sprinkle salt and pepper in cavity.

Cook spinach, drain and squeeze out excess water.

In frying pan, brown bacon and onions together until bacon is crisp. Stir in mushrooms. Drain off excess fat and stir in cheese and spinach. Add salt and pepper to taste.

Stuff salmon, fold sides together, secure with skewers, brush with oil and place on baking sheet.

Bake on second rack from top in preheated 450°F oven for 10 minutes per inch thickness of stuffed salmon (measure at thickest point).

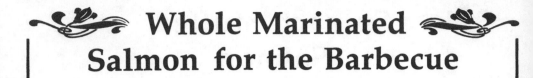

Whole Marinated Salmon for the Barbecue

An excellent recipe — will convert those who don't like salmon!

1 whole salmon

Marinade:

¼ lb. melted butter
4 oz. bottled honey 'n' garlic sauce
8 oz. bottled oyster sauce
6 oz. bottled teriyaki sauce
3-4 cloves garlic, minced
dash tabasco sauce
dash worcestershire sauce
1 tsp. dry mustard

Prepare marinade by combining all the ingredients.

Early in the day, butterfly and fillet salmon, leaving the skin on. Brush marinade on both sides, then place skin side down in glass dish and cover with lots of marinade. Refrigerate and brush on marinade several times during the day.

When time to barbecue, place salmon in a hamburger patty rack or fish rack. Cook skin side first to sear it. Turn it over and cook until done. Do not overcook.

(Any leftover marinade can be refrigerated or frozen.)

Eggs and Cheeses

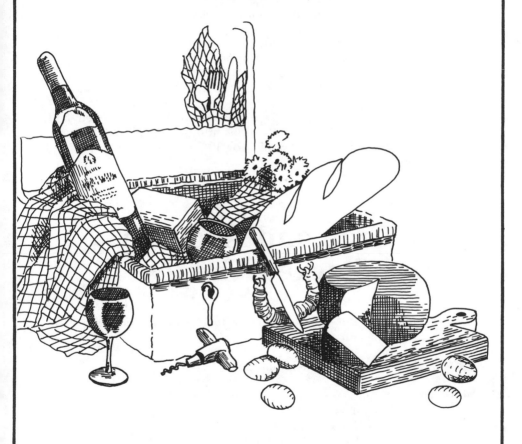

A luncheon dish made in the blender. Serve in individual ramekins with a crisp green salad and cornmeal bacon muffins (p.78).

5 eggs
1 cup creamed cottage cheese
¼ cup butter, melted and cooled
¼ cup flour
½ tsp. baking powder
1 can green chilies, chopped, hot or mild
   as to your taste
8 oz. monterey jack cheese, grated

Put all ingredients in blender except chilies and cheese. Mix well, add chilies and cheese and blend slightly. Pour into individual buttered ramekins or a casserole. Bake at 350°F for 30-35 minutes. Serve immediately.

This recipe can be doubled.

Crab and Avocado Stacked Crêpes

Time consuming, but well worth the effort! A unique luncheon dish.

Prepare 13 crêpes, 7 inches in diameter.

Sauce:

1 cup sour cream
1 clove garlic, minced
4 tbsp. parsley, chopped
½ tsp. salt
2 tbsp. lemon juice

Mix well in small bowl.

Mushroom layer:

3 tbsp. butter
½ lb. fresh mushrooms, sliced
1 small onion, chopped
salt and pepper to taste

Melt butter in frying pan and sauté mushrooms and onion until onion is limp. Season with salt and pepper.

Crab layer:

>1½ cups fresh or canned crab meat

Set aside 5 to 6 pieces of crab for garnish.

Avocado layer:

>2-3 medium ripe avocados
>lemon juice

Cut avocados into ⅛ inch pieces and drizzle with lemon juice to prevent browning. Set aside 5-6 pieces for garnish.

Assemble:
First crêpe — Spread a crêpe with about ¾ tbsp. sour cream mixture and place it on a shallow round heatproof dish. Spread ¼ of the mushroom mixture evenly over crêpe to outside edges.
Second crêpe — Spread a second crêpe with ¾ tbsp. sour cream mixture and set it on top of first crêpe. Spread ¼ of the crab over it.
Third crêpe — Spread a third crêpe with ¾ tbsp. sour cream mixture, and top with ¼ of the avocado.
Repeat these 3 layers, 3 more times. Then place 13th crêpe on top. If made ahead, cover and chill.
To serve — place crêpe stack, loosely covered with foil, in a 375°F oven until heated through — about 20-25 minutes. (If taken directly from the refrigerator, cook about 40 minutes). Garnish top with remaining avocado and crab. Pass remaining sour cream mixture at table. Cut into wedges to serve.

Serves 5-6.

Barbara's Crab Soufflé

Another nice luncheon dish, make the day ahead.

4 slices white bread, left whole
4 slices white bread, cubed
½ cup mayonnaise
1 cup celery, chopped
1 green pepper, chopped
1 medium onion, chopped
2 cups fresh crab or 2 - 7½ oz. canned crab
4 eggs, beaten
3 cups milk

Topping:

1 - 10 oz. can cream of mushroom soup
grated cheddar cheese, to cover top
paprika

Place 4 whole slices bread in large casserole or use both a 9" × 13" and an 8' × 8" pan.

Mix cubed bread, mayonnaise, celery, pepper, onion and crab together. Spread over bread in baking dish.

Beat eggs and milk together and pour over crab mixture.

Cover and refrigerate overnight.

Bake uncovered at 325°F for 15 minutes. Take out and top with soup, cheese and paprika and bake for 1 hour.

(Do not fill pans more than half full as mixture puffs up and overflows.)

Serves 8.

Creamy Poached Eggs

Try this with our English Muffin in a Loaf (p.78).

1 cup milk
¾ cup sharp cheddar cheese, grated
¼ cup stuffed green olives, sliced
1 tbsp. butter
1 tsp. chives, chopped
dash tabasco
1 tbsp. flour
½ cup sour cream
4 eggs
2 English muffins, split, toasted and buttered

In frying pan, combine milk, cheese, olives, butter, chives and tabasco. Cook over medium heat and stir until cheese is melted.

In a small bowl combine flour and sour cream and blend into hot milk mixture. Stir until bubbly.

Break one egg into a saucer. Make a swirl in simmering milk mixture and slip egg into middle of swirl. Repeat 3 more times. Cover and simmer 3-4 minutes.

Serve on English muffins with lots of sauce.

Serves 2-4.

Poached Eggs in Cream

A great, late breakfast.

3 raw potatoes or 3 previously baked potatoes
4 tbsp. melted butter
salt and pepper to taste
dash nutmeg
⅓ cup Gruyère cheese, grated
6 eggs
salt and pepper to taste
1 cup whipping cream

Cut potatoes into thin slices and sauté in melted butter until tender and browned on both sides. Season with salt and pepper and nutmeg.

Spread cooked potatoes on bottom of buttered baking dish and sprinkle with grated cheese. Break eggs on top of cheese. Add salt and pepper to taste and cover eggs with the cream.

Bake at 375°F for about 10 minutes or until eggs are set.

Serves 3-6.

No Crust
Mushroom Vegetable Pie

½ cup onion, chopped
1 cup zucchini, chopped
½ cup tomato, chopped
2 cups fresh mushrooms, sliced
1½ cups swiss cheese, grated

¾ cup milk
3 eggs
⅓ cup flour
1½ tsp. baking powder
1½ tbsp. vegetable oil
½ tsp. pepper
⅓ tsp. basil
½ tsp. salt

Italian herbs

   Grease a 10″ pie plate. Mix together onion, zucchini and tomato.
Spread mixture over bottom of pie plate and cover with mushrooms and
grated cheese.
   Place remaining ingredients, except Italian herbs, in blender and mix
well. Pour over vegetable mixture in pie plate and sprinkle with Italian
herbs. Bake at 400°F for 30 minutes or until set. Serve immediately.

Serves 6.

Onion Tart

A luncheon or vegetable side dish.

1 - 9 inch partially baked pie shell

½ cup butter
8 cups onions, chopped or finely sliced
1 tsp. salt and pepper to taste
½ tsp. ground cumin
4 eggs
½ cup sour cream
1 cup marbled cheese, grated

In frying pan melt butter and sauté onion, stirring frequently until tender and golden brown. Remove from heat and stir in salt, pepper and cumin.

In small bowl, beat eggs with sour cream until well blended. Add cheese and stir.

Add egg mixture to onion mixture. Turn into pie shell.

Bake at 425°F for 35 minutes.

6-8 servings.

 # Spinach Crêpes

Buy a chunk of fresh Italian parmesan and grate it yourself at home — you'll notice the difference! These crêpes can be made ahead and reheated.

Crêpe batter (can be made in blender)
> 4 eggs
> 1 cup milk
> 1 tsp. salt
> 1 cup flour
> ½ cup butter, melted

Filling — for 10-12 crêpes
> 2 pkgs. frozen spinach, chopped thawed and drained
> 2 tbsp. butter
> 4 cups white sauce, homemade
> 2 cups Italian parmesan cheese, freshly grated
> salt and pepper to taste

Crepes: Beat eggs until fluffy. Add milk and salt and continue to beat while sprinkling with flour. Pour in melted butter and beat thoroughly. Cover and chill 1 hour. Batter will have the consistency of heavy cream.

Filling: Sauté spinach in butter for 2 minutes and then add ½ of the white sauce. Add ½ of the cheese and stir well. When cheese has melted remove from heat and divide spinach mixture evenly among 10 to 12 crêpes. Roll up crêpes and keep warm in ovenproof dish. Combine remaining white sauce with remaining cheese and pour over crêpes. Heat through in oven.

Serves 10-12 as an appetizer, 5-6 as a luncheon dish.

Breads

Savory

Anne's Nova Scotia Oat Cakes

1 cup butter
1 cup Crisco shortening
1 cup sugar
¼ cup water
3 cups flour
1 tsp. salt
3 cups oatmeal

Cream butter, shortening, sugar and water together in a large bowl. Add flour, salt and oatmeal and mix well. Roll mixture out to ¼ inch thickness. Cut into 3 inch circles or pat onto cookie sheets and mark into squares.
Bake at 375°F for 15 minutes.

Quick Cheese Bread

2 cups flour
1 tsp. dry mustard
4 tsp. baking powder
1 tbsp. sugar
½ tsp. salt
2 cups cheddar cheese, grated
1 egg, beaten
¼ cup butter, melted
¾ cup milk

Sift together dry ingredients. Add cheese and mix. Blend egg, butter and milk together and mix with dry ingredients. Put into greased loaf pan and bake at 350°F for 45 minutes or until done.

 # Brioche In A Loaf

Use a food processor for this butter and egg bread.

1 tbsp. yeast
¼ cup warm milk
1 tbsp. sugar
2 cups flour
1 tsp. salt
½ cup hard butter, cut into 8 pieces
2 eggs, lightly beaten

Dissolve yeast in warm milk with sugar. Add flour, salt and butter to processor, and process for about 20 seconds or until butter is cut into flour mixture. Add yeast mixture and process about 5 seconds. Add eggs and process until ball of dough forms on blades. Place on lightly floured board and knead 1 to 2 minutes. Put in a greased bowl, cover and let rise in warm place for approximately 1½ to 2 hours. Punch down, knead several times and shape into a greased loaf pan.

Cover and let rise for 1 hour.
Bake at 350°F for 35 minutes.

Jean's Baking Powder Biscuits

Treat gently — don't over mix!

2 cups flour
½ tsp. salt
4 tsp. baking powder
1 tbsp. sugar
½ cup margarine or butter
1 cup milk

Mix flour, salt, baking powder and sugar in a bowl. Cut in butter. Add milk and mix gently until moistened. Place dough on lightly floured board and knead gently. Sprinkle with flour between each kneading until stickiness is gone.

Pat dough to ¾ inch thickness and cut into squares or triangles.
Bake at 425°F for 10-12 minutes.

Serve hot with butter and jam.

Bacon, Onion, Poppy Seed, Cheese Bread

½ lb. bacon, cooked and crumbled
1 tbsp. bacon drippings
1 cup onions, chopped
1½ cups flour
1 tbsp. baking powder
½ cup margarine
1 egg, beaten
½ cup milk
1 cup nippy cheddar cheese, grated

Topping:

1-2 tbsp. butter, melted
¼ cup poppy seeds
½ cup cheese, grated

Sauté onion in reserved bacon drippings.

Sift together flour and baking powder and cut in margarine. Stir in egg and milk. Add cheese, onions and bacon. Spread in a greased 8" × 8" pan.

Topping: drizzle butter over top. Sprinkle with poppy seeds and cheese.

Bake at 400°F for 20 minutes or until done.

Cut into squares.

Good hot or cold.

Cornmeal, Bacon Muffins or Loaf

6 strips bacon, cooked and crumbled
1½ cups cornmeal
1 cup flour
⅓ cup sugar
1 tsp. salt
1 tbsp. baking powder
2 eggs
6 tbsp. butter, melted and cooled
8 tbsp. oil
1½ cups milk

Sift dry ingredients. In a bowl, beat eggs slightly, add butter, oil and milk. Add dry ingredients and mix together until smooth.

Pour half of batter into greased muffin or loaf tin, sprinkle with half the bacon, top with remaining batter and sprinkle with remaining bacon.

Bake at 375°F for 30 minutes for loaf or 15-20 minutes for muffins.

Wendy's English Muffin in a Loaf

1 tbsp. sugar
2 tbsp. yeast
½ cup warm water
2 cups milk
2 tsp. salt
6 cups flour
¼ tsp. baking soda
½ lb. strong cheddar cheese, grated

cornmeal

In a large bowl, dissolve sugar and yeast in warm water. Heat milk, add salt and blend into the yeast mixture. Add 3 cups of flour and baking soda and mix well.

Add remaining 3 cups of flour to make a stiff batter. Add cheese and mix well again.

Divide batter in half and press into 2 loaf pans that have been greased

and sprinkled with cornmeal.

Sprinkle tops with cornmeal. Cover and let rise in warm place for 45 minutes.

Bake at 400°F for 25-30 minutes.

Cut thinly, toast, and serve with butter.

Graham Bread

A quick bread!

> 2 cups graham flour
> 1 cup all purpose flour
> ½ cup sugar
> pinch of salt
> 2 tsp. baking soda
> 2 cups buttermilk

Sift together dry ingredients except for baking soda. Stir baking soda into buttermilk and add to dry ingredients. Mix well.

Pour into a greased loaf pan and bake at 375°F for 45 minutes.

This recipe can be doubled.

No Knead
Dill Bread

Everyone asks for this recipe!

> 1 tbsp. yeast
> ¼ cup warm water
> 1 cup creamed cottage cheese
> 2 tbsp. butter
> 3 tbsp. liquid honey
> 1 tsp. dried onion soup mix
> 2 tsp. dill weed
> ¼ tsp. baking soda
> 1 tsp. salt
> 1 egg, beaten
> 2½ cups flour

In a large bowl, dissolve yeast in warm water.

In a saucepan, warm the cottage cheese, butter and honey. Add onion soup mix, dill weed, baking soda, salt and egg. Stir to blend. Add cottage cheese mixture to yeast and stir well. Add flour to make firm ball of dough. Cover and let rise in warm place, for about 1 hour.

Stir the dough down. Shape dough into a greased loaf pan. Cover and let rise about 1 hour.

Bake at 350°F for 30 minutes or until golden brown.

This recipe doubles and freezes well!

Photo: Rhubarb Bread, page 88.

One Hour
Food Processor Buns

A cross between a baking powder biscuit and a yeast bun.

1 tbsp. yeast
½ cup milk, warmed
2¼ cups flour
½ tsp. salt
1½ tbsp. sugar
2 heaping tbsp. butter
¼ cup hot water

Dissolve yeast in warm milk. Set aside. Measure flour, salt, sugar and butter in food processor. Process 15 seconds or until butter is mixed in. Add water to yeast mixture and pour into processor. Process until dough becomes one lump.

Take out dough and knead one minute. Put into greased bowl and cover. Let rise in warm place for 15 minutes (a 140°F oven is great). Remove dough from oven if rising there and heat oven to 425°F.

Shape dough into 12 small buns. Place side by side on greased cookie sheet. Slash top of buns. Cover and let rise in warm place for 15 minutes.

Bake at 425°F for 12 minutes.

Makes 12 small buns or 1 large pizza crust.

Ricotta Cheese
Herb Bread

Better than good — this is great! Double this and freeze one loaf.

¼ cup milk, scalded and cooled to lukewarm
1 tbsp. yeast
1 tbsp. sugar
6 tbsp. butter, softened
2 eggs
2 tsp. salt
1½ cups ricotta cheese
2 tbsp. fresh parsley, snipped
2 tbsp. fresh chives, snipped
½ tsp. dried marjoram
1 tsp. dried basil
1 tsp. dried rosemary
1 tsp. dried oregano
3-4 cups flour

1 egg yolk blended with 2 tbsp. milk

Stir milk, yeast and sugar in a large mixer bowl until yeast dissolves.
Beat in butter, eggs and salt until smooth. Blend in ricotta cheese and
herbs. Beat in 3 cups of flour until smooth (about 5 minutes). If mixture
appears too moist, beat in up to 1 more cup of flour. Dough should be
soft but not dry. Transfer to buttered bowl. Cover and let rise in warm
place for about 1½ hours.
    Punch down and let rise again until doubled.
    Shape dough into a greased loaf pan. Let rise in a warm place.
    Brush with egg glaze. Bake at 375°F for 40-50 minutes.

 # Eileen's Scotch Scones

1 tsp. baking soda
1 cup buttermilk
2¼ - 2½ cups flour
2 tsp. cream of tartar
pinch of salt
¼ cup lard
2 tbsp. Roger's golden syrup

8 tbsp. butter

Add baking soda to buttermilk and set aside.

Sift dry ingredients. Add lard and cut in until crumbly. Add syrup and buttermilk-soda mixture and mix lightly.

Place on a floured board and shape into a circle one inch thick. Cut into 8 triangles.

Melt 4 tbsp. butter in frying pan. Brown triangles on one side for 5 minutes or until lightly browned. Add 4 more tbsp. of butter and brown other side of triangles. Brown edges by standing on edge.

Serve hot with butter.

 # Mom's Scones

Good warm from the oven with butter and jam!

3 cups flour
½ cup sugar
2 tsp. baking powder
1 tsp. baking soda
½ tsp. salt
¼ cup butter
¼ cup Crisco shortening
1 egg, beaten
¼ cup milk
1 cup raisins

Sift together dry ingredients. Cut in butter and shortening until crumbly. Add egg and milk and mix together. (If dough is too stiff, add more milk.) Mix in raisins.

Drop dough by large spoonfuls onto a greased cookie sheet.

Bake at 350°F for 12-15 minutes or until brown.

For cheese scones, add less sugar, omit raisins and add 1 cup of grated cheddar cheese.

Loaves

Apple Cheddar Bread

2 cups flour
⅔ cup sugar
½ tsp. cinnamon
1 tsp. baking powder
1 tsp. salt
½ cup walnuts or pecans, chopped
2 eggs
½ cup salad oil
1½ cups apples, diced
½ cup sharp cheddar cheese, grated
½ cup milk

Combine dry ingredients in bowl. Mix together remaining ingredients and add to dry ingredients. Mix well. Spoon into a greased loaf pan.
Bake one hour at 350°F.

Apple Bread

1 cup sugar
1 tsp. cinnamon
1½ cups flour
1 tsp. baking soda
¼ tsp. salt
1 egg
½ cup corn oil
2 generous cups of apples, diced
1 cup pecans, chopped

Combine dry ingredients in a bowl. Beat egg and oil together and add to dry ingredients along with apples and pecans. Spoon mixture into a greased loaf pan. Bake at 350°F for 1 hour.

Apricot - Bran Bread

Serve this in place of muffins — not a sweet bread.

¾ cup water
¾ cup dried apricots (chopped)
½ cup raisins
¾ cup bran
1¼ cups flour
½ cup brown sugar
1 tsp. baking powder
½ tsp. baking soda
½ tsp. salt

2 eggs
¼ cup oil
1 tsp. vanilla

Combine water, apricots and raisins in saucepan. Bring mixture to boil, remove from heat and stir in bran. Cool for 10 minutes.
Combine dry ingredients and set aside.
Beat eggs until frothy, add oil and vanilla. Stir into apricot mixture.
Add dry ingredients and mix until well blended. Pour into greased loaf pan.
Bake at 350°F for 50-55 minutes.

 # Barb's Blueberry -
Cheese Bread

2 cups flour
1 cup sugar
1½ tsp. baking powder
½ tsp. baking soda
1 tsp. salt
1 tbsp. orange rind, grated
1 cup sharp cheddar cheese, grated
¾ cup orange juice
2 tbsp. margarine, melted
1 egg
1 cup fresh or frozen blueberries

Combine flour, sugar, baking powder, soda, salt, orange rind and cheese and mix together. Add juice, shortening and egg. Beat until smooth. Carefully fold in blueberries. Pour into a well greased 1½ quart baking dish. (Round is great.)

Bake at 350°F for 55-65 minutes or until bread is firm to touch.

Pumpkin Loaf

Wonderfully moist — what can you make when the cupboard is bare?

1½ cups flour
½ cup Mazola oil, or melted margarine
1 cup sugar
2 eggs, beaten
1 tsp. baking soda
1 tsp. baking powder
1 tsp. cinnamon (not for bananas)*
pinch of salt
1 cup pumpkin or apple sauce
   or 1½ cups mashed bananas
1 cup raisins

Combine all ingredients and blend well. Pour into a greased loaf pan and bake at 350°F for 45-55 minutes.

* Mix bananas with soda and substitute vanilla for cinnamon.

 # Rhubarb Bread

Best made with fresh rhubarb. Makes 2 loaves.
See picture opposite page 80.

1½ cups brown sugar, packed
⅔ cup oil
1 egg
1 cup sour milk*　⎫
1 tsp. baking soda　⎬　mix together
1 tsp. vanilla　　　⎭
2½ cups flour
2 cups fresh rhubarb, cubed
1 cup nuts, chopped

Topping:

½ cup sugar
½ tsp. cinnamon
1 tbsp. butter

Mix sugar, oil, and egg together. Add sour milk to which the baking soda has been added. Add remaining ingredients and blend well.

Pour batter into 2 greased loaf pans.

Topping: Mix ingredients together and sprinkle on loaves.
Bake at 325°F for 50-60 minutes.

* To make sour milk, add 1 tsp. lemon juice & vinegar to 1 cup milk.

We like to double this recipe and freeze the extra loaves.

Muffins

Marj's Bran Muffins

½ cup margarine, softened
2 tbsp. molasses
⅓ cup brown sugar, packed
2 eggs, beaten
1 cup flour
1 tsp. baking soda
½ tsp. cinnamon
¼ tsp. nutmeg
¼ tsp. salt
1 cup buttermilk
1 cup natural bran
1 cup dates or raisins

In large bowl, mix margarine, molasses, brown sugar and beaten eggs.
Sift dry ingredients and add to molasses mixture. Gently mix in buttermilk, bran and fruit.
Pour into greased muffin tins and bake at 400°F for 17½ minutes.

Makes 12 large muffins.
This recipe can be doubled or tripled.

Auntie Helen's
Carrot and Pineapple Muffins

1 cup sugar
2 eggs
⅔ cup oil
1 cup carrots, grated
¾ cup crushed pineapple, undrained
½ tsp. vanilla
1½ cups flour
½ tsp. salt
1 tsp. baking soda
1 tsp. baking powder
½ tsp. cinnamon

In a large bowl cream together sugar, eggs and oil. Add carrots, pineapple and vanilla.

Sift together dry ingredients and add to wet ingredients and gently blend.

Pour into greased muffin tins and bake at 400°F for 15 to 18 minutes.

Orange and Date Muffins

Food processor muffins.

1½ cups flour
1 tsp. baking powder
1 tsp. baking soda
1 tsp. salt
½ cup pitted dates
¾ cup sugar
1 unpeeled orange, cut into chunks and seeded
½ cup butter
1 large egg
½ cup orange juice

Process flour, baking powder, baking soda and salt for about 5 seconds. Transfer to another bowl.

Process the dates with sugar until the dates are coarsely chopped. Add the orange pieces and pulse until finely chopped. Add butter, egg and orange juice and process for 25 seconds to blend well. Add the

reserved dry ingredients and mix with wooden spoon until just blended. Do not over beat. Pour into greased muffin tins.
Bake at 400°F for 15 minutes.

Makes 12 large muffins.

Raspberry Muffins

Yummy topping of cinnamon, sugar and oatmeal.

Muffins:

1½ cups flour
½ cup oatmeal
½ cup brown sugar, packed
¼ tsp. salt
2 tsp. baking powder
1 tsp. baking soda
1 cup (or more) frozen raspberries (do not thaw)
2 eggs
½ cup buttermilk
½ cup margarine, melted

Topping:

¼ cup butter, softened
¼ cup brown sugar
¼ cup oatmeal
¼ cup flour
1 tsp. cinnamon

Muffins: In a large bowl, mix flour, oatmeal, sugar, baking powder and baking soda. Add frozen raspberries and stir to coat.
In a small bowl, beat eggs and stir in buttermilk and margarine. Add liquid ingredients to flour mixture and stir until just blended.

Topping: Mix together all ingredients until crumbly.
Fill greased muffin tins ⅔ full. Top with cinnamon topping.
Bake at 400°F for 15-20 minutes.

Sugar Jam Muffins

Taste like sugary doughnuts. Recipe can be easily doubled or tripled.

½ cup sugar
½ cup butter or margarine
1 egg, beaten
½ cup milk
1½ cup flour
1½ tsp. baking powder
jam

butter, melted

½ cup sugar
½ tsp. cinnamon } Mix together

In a small bowl, cream sugar and butter until smooth. Add egg and milk and blend well. In a medium bowl sift dry ingredients and gently mix in the egg mixture until just blended.

Spoon half the dough into the bottom of eight greased muffin tins and place a dab of jam in the middle of each muffin. Top with rest of batter and bake at 400°F for 15 to 18 minutes.

While still warm, dip each muffin in melted butter and roll in cinnamon sugar.

Makes 8 large muffins.

Blueberry, Buttermilk Teacakes

2 cups flour
½ cup sugar
1 tbsp. baking powder
1 tsp. orange peel, grated
1 tsp. salt
¼ tsp. baking soda
⅓ cup Crisco shortening
¾ cup buttermilk
1 egg, beaten
1 cup frozen blueberries (do not thaw)

3 tbsp. butter, melted
3 tbsp. sugar
¼ tsp. cinnamon
⅛ tsp. nutmeg

In a large bowl, combine first 6 ingredients. Cut in shortening until mixture resembles coarse meal.

Combine buttermilk and egg and mix into dry ingredients. Stir in blueberries.

Gently knead on floured surface 5 to 6 times. Pat to ½ inch thickness and cut into 2 to 3 inch circles. Place on greased cookie sheet.

Bake at 400°F for 20 minutes.

Combine melted butter, sugar, cinnamon and nutmeg and brush over warm teacakes. Serve immediately.

Makes 12 teacakes.

 # Welsh Teacakes

Make these teacakes small and serve with butter and jam.

3 cups flour
1 tbsp. baking powder
½ tsp. salt
1 cup sugar
1 cup margarine or butter
1 cup currants
2 eggs, beaten
¼ cup milk

butter for frying

Sift dry ingredients into a large bowl. Cut in margarine or butter until mixture resembles coarse meal. Add currants, eggs and milk and blend. (This makes a fairly stiff dough.)

On a floured board, roll out dough to ¼-½ inch thickness and cut into 2 inch circles.

In melted butter fry at medium to high heat for 4 to 6 minutes on each side. Watch carefully.

 # Desserts

Sheila's
Chocolate Chip Cookies

A crispy version of an old favorite.

1 cup margarine, softened
1 cup brown sugar, packed
1 cup white sugar
1 egg
1 tbsp. milk
2 tsp. vanilla
3½ cups flour
3 tsp. soda
1 tsp. salt
1 cup vegetable oil
1 cup cornflakes, crushed
1 cup oatmeal
1 - 12 oz. pkg. chocolate chips

Beat margarine, sugars, egg, milk and vanilla until well blended. Stir in flour, soda and salt alternately with the oil. Blend in cornflakes, oatmeal and chocolate chips. Drop by rounded teaspoons on to an ungreased cookie sheet. Flatten with fork.
Bake at 350°F for 10 to 12 minutes.

Variation - add 2-3 smarties on top of each cookie before baking.
To make ice cream sandwiches, make extra large cookies and fill with ice cream. Freeze.

Makes 7 dozen.

 # Dad's Favourite Cookies

Old fashioned, chewy goodness!

1 cup shortening
1 cup white sugar
½ cup brown sugar
1 egg
1½ cups flour
1 tsp. baking soda
1 tsp. nutmeg
1 tsp. baking powder
1½ tsp. cinnamon
1 tsp. vanilla
2 tbsp. molasses
1½ cups oatmeal
1 cup coconut, long shredded

Cream shortening and sugars well, add egg and beat until well blended.

Sift dry ingredients, except oatmeal and coconut. Add dry ingredients to shortening mixture and blend well. Stir in vanilla, molasses, oatmeal and coconut.

Drop by large tablespoons on a greased cookie sheet, two inches apart. Do not press down.

Bake at 300°F for 20 minutes or until brown.

Ethel's Ginger Cookies

A soft ginger cookie — chill batter overnight before baking.

¾ cup butter
1 cup sugar
1 egg
¼ cup molasses
2¼ cups flour
½ tsp. salt
1 tsp. cinnamon
1 tbsp. ginger
1 tsp. baking soda

sugar

Cream butter, sugar and egg together. Add molasses and blend thoroughly.

Sift flour, salt, cinnamon, ginger and baking soda together and add to the butter mixture. Mix well. Chill overnight in refrigerator.

Shape dough into small balls and roll in granulated sugar. On a greased baking sheet, flatten each cookie with thumb.

Bake at 350°F for 12 to 15 minutes.

Chocolate Gingerbreadmen

½ cup Crisco shortening
½ cup molasses
2 squares unsweetened chocolate
2½ cups flour
⅔ cup sugar
1 tsp. baking powder
1 tsp. ginger
¼ tsp. salt
¼ cup milk

Melt shortening, molasses and chocolate in top of double boiler. Cool. In a large bowl, sift dry ingredients. Add chocolate mixture and milk

to dry ingredients and blend well. Refrigerate dough until well chilled.

Roll out dough on lightly floured board to ¼ inch thickness. Cut into gingerbreadmen, place on cookie sheet and press in decorations.

Bake at 375°F for 8 minutes.

Roné's Gingerbreadmen

1 cup butter
1½ cups sugar
1 egg
4 tsp. orange peel, grated
2 tbsp. corn syrup
3 cups flour
2 tsp. baking soda
2 tsp. cinnamon
1 tsp. ginger
½ tsp. salt
½ tsp. cloves

In a large bowl, cream butter and sugar. Add egg, orange peel and corn syrup and mix until well blended.

Sift dry ingredients together and add to butter mixture. Mix well. Chill dough thoroughly.

On lightly floured board, roll dough to ¼ inch thickness. Cut out gingerbreadmen and place on ungreased cookie sheet.

Bake at 375°F for 8-10 minutes.

Raisins and smarties may be pressed into dough before baking, or cool and decorate.

 # Granola Cookies

1 cup butter or margarine
¾ cup granulated sugar
¾ cup brown sugar, packed
1 egg
1 tsp. vanilla
1½ cups flour
1 tsp. salt
1 tsp. baking soda
1¾ cups granola
1 cup raisins
½ cup baking peanuts, chopped

Cream butter and sugars. Add egg and vanilla and beat well.
Mix together flour, salt and baking soda and add to creamed mixture.
Blend well. Add granola, raisins and peanuts.
Drop by teaspoons onto a greased cookie sheet.
Bake at 375°F for 10-12 minutes.

Variations: -

a) 1 - 6 oz. pkg. chocolate chips instead of raisins.
b) 1 cup chopped dates instead of raisins.

Oatmeal Lace Cookies

1½ cups flour
1 tsp. baking soda
1 tsp. salt
1½ cups butter, room temperature
1½ cups brown sugar, packed
1 cup granulated sugar
2 eggs
1 tsp. vanilla
2½ cups oatmeal
1½ cups walnuts, finely chopped

Sift together flour, baking soda and salt and set aside.
In a large bowl, beat butter with sugars until smooth and fluffy. Add
eggs one at a time beating well and then add vanilla. Gradually add

flour mixture and mix well. Stir in oatmeal and walnuts.

Drop by rounded teaspoons, 2 inches apart, onto a ungreased cookie sheet.

Bake at 350°F for 12 minutes.

Makes approximately 7 dozen cookies.

Pebe's Greek Shortbread

Melts in your mouth!

1 lb. butter, softened
1½ tbsp. vanilla
¾ cup icing sugar
3 to 4 cups flour

icing sugar, sifted

In the large bowl of a mixer, add butter, vanilla and icing sugar and beat for 30 minutes. Add enough flour, usually about 4 cups, to make a soft dough. (Do not add too much flour as cookies will become dry). Pat out the dough to ¼ inch thickness on lightly floured board. Cut dough into squares. Carefully place cookies on cookie sheet and bake at 350°F for 7 to 8 minutes. Watch closely.

While cookies are still warm, dip into sifted icing sugar.

Makes approximately 7 dozen cookies.

Almond Checkerboard Slice

1 - 8" × 8" sheet of pastry
2-3 tbsp. strawberry or raspberry jam

½ cup butter
⅔ cup sugar
2 eggs
⅔ cup rice flour
¼ tsp. salt
1 tsp. almond extract
red and green food colouring

Place pastry in an 8" × 8" baking dish. Spread jam on pastry. Set aside.

Cream butter and sugar together, add eggs and mix well. Mix in flour, salt and almond extract.

Divide batter in half, add a few drops of green food colouring to one half and a few drops of red food colouring to the other half. Put teaspoons of batter alternately on pastry jam bottom to cover. (This will make a checkerboard effect.)

Bake at 375°F for 35 minutes.

Ice with pink butter icing.

Butter Icing

3 tbsp. butter
1 tsp. vanilla
3 tbsp. hot milk
2 cups icing sugar
few drops red food colouring

Cream butter, add vanilla and milk alternately with icing sugar. Beat until smooth. Add food colouring to make pink icing.

Spread on cooled almond slice.

 # Almond Roca Square

Can't leave it alone!

1 cup butter, melted
1 cup brown sugar, packed
1½ cups flour
1 tsp. almond extract
1½ cups semi-sweet chocolate chips
1½ cups almonds, roasted and chopped

Melt butter, add brown sugar, flour and almond extract. Press into a 9" × 13" baking dish and bake at 350°F for 20 minutes. Remove from oven and immediately sprinkle with chocolate chips. Spread the melted chips and top with roasted almonds. Press lightly.

Caramel Nut Brownies

Gooey and yummy!

50 caramels (14 oz. pkg.)
⅔ cups evaporated milk
1 German chocolate cake mix
¾ cup melted butter
1 cup chocolate chips
1 cup pecans, chopped

Melt caramels with ⅓ cup milk in top of double boiler. Stir often. Set aside and keep warm.
Combine cake mix with melted butter and remaining ⅓ cup milk.
Spread half of this mixture into a greased 9" × 13" inch pan.
Bake at 350°F for 6-8 minutes.
Remove from oven and sprinkle with chocolate chips and pecans. Drizzle melted caramels over chips and nuts. Cover with remaining cake batter.
Bake at 350°F for additional 15 minutes or until brownies are firm to touch.
Cool before cutting.

Candied Fruit Slice

A shortbread crust, tangy fruit centre and tart lemon icing.

Base:

½ cup butter
3 tbsp. sugar
1½ cups flour
1 tsp. vanilla
pinch of salt

Filling:

2 eggs
1 cup brown sugar
3 tbsp. flour
1 tsp. baking powder
1 tsp. lemon juice
1 tsp. lemon rind
½ cup raisins
1 - 8 oz. pkg. candied fruit

Base: Cream butter and sugar, add flour, vanilla and salt and blend well. Press into an 8" × 8" pan and bake at 350°F for 10 minutes. Remove from oven and reduce oven temp. to 300°F.

Filling: Beat eggs, add brown sugar and blend well. Add flour, baking powder, lemon juice and rind and blend. Stir in raisins and candied fruit. Spread on top of baked shortbread crust and bake at 300°F for 35 to 45 minutes or until firm and golden brown. When cool, ice with lemon icing.

Lemon Icing:

3 tbsp. butter
2 tsp. lemon juice
½ tsp. vanilla
2 cups icing sugar
2-3 tbsp. hot milk

Cream butter, add lemon juice and vanilla. Add icing sugar and hot milk alternately and beat until smooth. Spread on cooled slice.

Chris' Favourite Cherry Chew Squares

Base:

1 cup flour
1 cup oatmeal
1 cup brown sugar
1 tsp. baking soda
¼ tsp. salt
½ cup butter, softened

Topping:

2 eggs, beaten
1 cup brown sugar
½ tsp. almond extract
2 tbsp. flour
1 tsp. baking powder
½ tsp. salt
1 cup coconut
1 cup well drained maraschino cherries, halved (reserve liquid)
½ cup pecans, chopped

Base: Mix flour, oatmeal, sugar, soda and salt. Add butter and mix until crumbly. Press mixture into greased 9" × 13" pan. Bake at 350°F for 10 minutes.

Topping: Stir sugar and almond extract into beaten eggs.

Mix together flour, baking powder and salt and stir into egg mixture. Add coconut and cherries and mix well. Pour over crust, spreading evenly. Sprinkle with pecans.

Bake at 350°F for 25 minutes or until lightly brown.

Cool and ice with cherry almond icing.

Icing:

⅓ cup butter
1½ cups icing sugar
½ tsp. almond extract
2 tbsp. cherry juice
few drops of hot water
2 drops of red food colouring

Cream butter and icing sugar together. Add almond extract, cherry juice, water, food colouring and beat until fluffy.

Cherry Cream Squares

Base:

1½ cups flour
¼ cup sugar
¾ cup butter, softened

Topping:

2 eggs
1 cup brown sugar
2 tbsp. flour
¼ tsp. baking powder
2 tsp. vanilla
1 cup maraschino cherries, chopped
½ cup pecans, chopped

Base: Sift flour and sugar together. Cut in butter until mixture is crumbly. Press into a greased 8" × 8" pan.
Bake at 350°F for 15 minutes.
Topping: Beat eggs and sugar together, mixing thoroughly. Sift flour and baking powder and mix into egg mixture. Stir in vanilla, cherries and nuts. Pour on top of the base and bake at 350°F for an additional 20-25 minutes or until firm.

Chocolate Fudge Peanut Butter Squares

No bake — chocolate decadence!

½ cup butter or margarine
1 cup peanut butter
1½ cups semi-sweet chocolate chips
2 cups miniature marshmallows

Melt butter, peanut butter and chocolate chips in top of a double boiler. Add marshmallows and mix well. Spread in a 8" × 8" greased pan and refrigerate.

Janie's Rice Krispie Squares

Base and Topping:

>1 cup butterscotch chips
>½ cup peanut butter
>4 cups rice krispies

Filling:

>1 tbsp. water
>1 cup chocolate chips
>½ cup icing sugar
>2 tbsp. butter, softened

Base: Melt the butterscotch chips and peanut butter over low heat and add the rice krispies. Press ½ of this mixture into a greased 8" × 8" pan. Refrigerate. Reserve remaining mixture.

Filling: In a small saucepan, melt filling ingredients. Pour the filling on top of rice krispie base and spread evenly. Press the reserved rice krispie mixture on top of filling. Refrigerate.

Walnut Squares

An old favourite!

Base:

>1 cup flour
>½ cup butter, softened

Filling:

>1¼ cups brown sugar
>2 eggs, beaten
>1 cup walnuts, coarsely chopped
>2 tbsp. flour
>pinch of salt
>½ tsp. baking powder
>½ cup coconut

Mix flour with butter until crumbly and press into an 8" × 8" pan.

Mix filling ingredients together and pour over base. Bake at 325°F for 40-45 minutes. Cool and ice with butter icing for unbaked wafer squares (p.110).

Louise's Raspberry Coconut Bars

Always good.

Base:

> 1 cup flour
> 1 tsp. baking powder
> ½ cup butter, softened
> 1 egg, well beaten
> 1 tsp. milk
>
> ½ cup raspberry jam

Topping:

> ½ cup butter, **softened**
> 1 cup sugar
> 1 egg, well beaten
> 1 tsp. vanilla
> 2 cups shredded sweetened coconut

Base: Mix flour and baking powder. Cut in butter until crumbly. Add egg and milk and blend well. Press into a greased 8" × 8" pan. Spread base with raspberry jam.

Topping: Cream butter and sugar. Add egg, vanilla and coconut. Mix well. Spread topping over jam.

Bake at 350°F for 45 minutes.

 # Sweet Marie Bars

No bake bars.

Base:

>   ½ cup brown sugar
>   ½ cup peanut butter
>   ½ cup corn syrup
>   2 cups rice krispies
>   1 cup peanuts, chopped

In a saucepan over medium heat, melt the sugar, peanut butter and corn syrup. Bring to a boil, stirring constantly. Take off heat quickly and add rice krispies and peanuts.

Press into a greased 8" × 8" pan and ice.

Icing:

>   3 tbsp. butter
>   3 tbsp. cocoa
>   2 tbsp. hot water
>   ½ tsp. vanilla
>   1½ cups icing sugar

Cream the butter and blend in the cocoa, hot water and vanilla. Add the icing sugar slowly and beat until creamy.

Unbaked Wafer Squares

Everybody likes this easy, unbaked square.

Base:

½ cup margarine
½ cup sugar
2 tbsp. cocoa
1 egg, well beaten
1 tsp. vanilla
½ cup walnuts, chopped
½ box graham wafers, coarsely broken

In a saucepan, melt margarine over medium heat. Add sugar and cocoa and mix well. Add egg and simmer for 1 minute, stirring constantly. Remove from heat and add vanilla, walnuts and broken graham wafers. Press into a greased 8″ × 8″ pan.

Butter Icing:

⅓ cup butter
1 tsp. vanilla
few drops hot water
1½ cups icing sugar

Cream the butter and blend in the rest of ingredients until fluffy.

Angel Food Torte

Heavenly!

Cake:

    1 - 10 inch prebaked angel food cake

Filling:

    1 - 7 oz. jar marshmallow cream
    1 tbsp. hot water
    1½ tsp. instant coffee powder
    1 tsp. vanilla
    1 cup whipping cream

Garnish:

    1 square semi-sweet chocolate, shaved
    2 tbsp. slivered almonds, toasted

In a bowl, combine marshmallow cream, water, coffee and vanilla. Beat until well blended and fluffy.

Whip cream and fold into marshmallow mixture.

Split cake crosswise into three layers. Frost each layer with marshmallow filling and sprinkle with shaved chocolate. Assemble layers on cake plate and top with almonds and shaved chocolate.

 # Apple Rum Cake

The rum sauce makes this cake special. Top with whipped cream laced with hazelnut liqueur.

3 eggs
½ lb. butter
¾ cup brown sugar, packed
1¼ cups flour
1 tsp. baking soda
½ tsp. salt
3 large apples, peeled, cored and thinly sliced
½ tsp. lemon peel, grated
1 tsp. cinnamon
½ tsp. ginger
1 tsp. vanilla
1 cup pecans, coarsely chopped

Mix eggs, butter and brown sugar together. Add flour, baking soda and salt. Set aside.

Slice 2 apples and sprinkle with lemon peel, cinnamon, ginger and vanilla and shake to coat. Stir apple mixture into butter mixture, add nuts and mix well. Spoon mixture into a greased tube pan and spread evenly. Slice remaining apple and decorate top in a circular fashion. Bake at 350°F for 40 to 45 minutes. Serve warm cake with hot rum sauce.

Rum Sauce:

1 cup whipping cream
½ cup white sugar
½ cup brown sugar
½ cup butter
½ cup rum

Combine cream and sugars in a saucepan and cook over low heat for 1 hour. Add butter and cook for another 30 minutes. Stir in rum. Serve hot over cake slices and top with whipped cream.

Photo: Di's Lemon Glazed Cheesecake, page 124.

 Blueberry Cobbler

An old-fashioned family dessert.

Cake:

    ¼ cup shortening
    ¼ cup sugar
    1 egg, well beaten
    1 cup flour
    ⅓ tsp. salt
    1½ tsp. baking powder
    ¼ cup milk
    ½ tsp. vanilla
    1½ cups fresh or frozen blueberries

Topping:

    ½ cup flour
    ⅛ tsp. salt
    2 tbsp. butter
    ½ cup sugar

Cake: Cream shortening and sugar together. Add egg and mix again.
Sift flour, salt and baking powder and add to shortening mixture.
Blend in milk and vanilla and beat until smooth. Spoon batter into a
greased 8" × 8" glass dish. Cover with blueberries.

Topping: Mix all ingredients until crumbly. Cover blueberries with the
topping and bake at 375°F for 30 minutes.

Sauce:

    1½ tbsp. flour
    ⅓ cup sugar
    ¼ tsp. salt
    ¾ cup water
    1 cup blueberries
    2 tsp. butter
    1 tbsp. lemon juice
    1 tsp. lemon peel, grated

Mix flour, sugar and salt in a saucepan. Add water and blueberries.
Cook over low heat until thickened and bubbly. Add butter, lemon juice
and peel and stir until butter is melted.

Serve warm sauce over warm cobbler.

113

Nathan's Carrot Cake with Cream Cheese Icing

In our cheesecake company, "Nathans," aside from making 20 varieties of cheesecakes, we also had a very popular carrot cake. Our customers loved it and so will you.

1 cup sugar
1 cup corn oil
3 eggs, beaten
1⅓ cups flour
1⅓ heaping tsp. baking powder
1⅓ heaping tsp. baking soda
1⅓ heaping tsp. cinnamon
½ tsp. salt
¾ cup raisins
¾ cup walnuts or pecans, chopped
½ cup coconut
2 cups carrots, grated

In large bowl, mix sugar, oil and eggs. Sift dry ingredients and add to egg mixture. Mix well. Blend in the raisins, nuts, coconut and carrot. Pour into a greased and lined tube pan.

Bake at 300°F for 1 hour and 15 minutes. (Slow oven makes this cake moist.)

Cream Cheese Icing:

4 oz. cream cheese, softened
4 oz. butter, softened
2 tsp. vanilla
2 cups icing sugar

Beat all ingredients together until smooth and creamy. Ice cooled carrot cake.

A very moist cake and freezes well.

Avril's Chocolate, Chocolate Chip Cake

Great for brown baggers and picnickers!

1 chocolate cake mix
1 - 3 oz. pkg. chocolate or vanilla instant pudding
1 cup sour cream
4 eggs
½ cup oil
½ cup water
12 oz. pkg. chocolate chips

Mix all ingredients except chocolate chips, and beat with electric beater for 2 minutes. Stir in chocolate chips.

Bake in a greased round tube or bundt pan at 350°F for exactly 1 hour.

No need to ice!

Di's Mom's
Chocolate Fudge Cake

A chocolate lover's snacking cake.

½ cup butter
2 squares unsweetened chocolate
1 cup boiling water
1 egg
1 cup sugar
1 tsp. vanilla
1¼ cup flour
1 heaping tsp. baking powder

Melt butter and chocolate in top of a double boiler. Add the boiling water and whisk well.

In a separate bowl, beat egg, sugar, and vanilla until blended.

On a piece of wax paper, sift the flour and baking powder together. Alternately add the chocolate mixture (in thirds) and the flour mixture (in thirds) to the egg mixture. Beat well after each addition. (This is a thin batter.) Pour into a greased 8″ pan and bake at 350°F for 30-35 minutes. Cool and ice with your favourite icing.

This is a small cake but the recipe can be doubled for a layer cake.

Hot Milk Sponge Cake
with Peanut Brittle Icing

3 eggs, well beaten
1 cup sugar
1 tsp. vanilla
1 cup cake flour
1 tsp. baking powder
6 tbsp. hot milk

Gradually add sugar to well beaten eggs. Beat until frothy and add vanilla. Sift flour and baking powder together, gently fold into egg

mixture. Stir in hot milk. Pour into an ungreased tube pan.
Bake at 350°F for 30-35 minutes or until top is firm.

Topping:

>2 cups whipping cream
>10 oz. pkg. of peanut brittle, crushed

Whip cream until stiff peaks form. Stir in peanut brittle and ice cake.

Variation: When cake is cool, slice in half horizontally. Spread fresh or frozen strawberries (raspberries or peaches) on bottom half and cover with top half. Ice with topping.

Mrs. Farquhar's Raisin Cake

>1½ cups raisins
>water
>¾ cup sugar
>⅓ cup butter
>1 egg
>1½ cup flour
>1 tsp. baking soda
>1 tsp. cinnamon
>1 tsp. nutmeg

Cover raisins with water in a small saucepan. Simmer 20 minutes. Cool. Drain raisins, reserving ½ cup of the raisin water.

In a medium bowl cream sugar and butter together. Add egg and beat. Mix together all the dry ingredients. Add flour mixture to sugar and butter mixture alternately with the raisin water. Mix in raisins. Pour into a greased bundt pan.

Bake at 325°F for 45 minutes or until done.

Ice if desired.

Mickey's Light Fruit Cake

Make 6 weeks before Christmas so that it may ripen.

4 cups flour
1 tsp. baking powder
1 tsp. cinnamon
1 tsp. nutmeg
1 lb. butter
2 cups sugar
10 eggs, beaten
1 lb. raisins
1 lb. currants
1 lb. mixed peel
½ lb. candied pineapple
½ lb. candied red cherries
½ lb. candied green cherries
1 cup orange juice

Sift together first four ingredients. Cream butter and sugar well, add beaten eggs. Sift half of the flour mixture over the fruit. Add remaining half to creamed mixture, then add fruit alternately with orange juice. Pour into well greased, brown paper lined large square wedding or Christmas cake pan.

Bake at 275°F for 3 hours or until a cake tester inserted in the centre comes out clean. Cool cake well before icing.

Almond Paste Icing:
2-3 tbsp. corn syrup
16 oz. almond paste
icing sugar

Melt corn syrup and brush top of cake.

Dust board with icing sugar and roll out almond paste to size of top of cake (will be approximately ½ inch thick). Place rolled almond paste on top of cake and press lightly to seal. Wrap cake well in Saran Wrap and then in aluminum foil. Ripen in well sealed cookie tin for 6 weeks or more.

Freezes indefinitely.

118

Raspberry Cobbler

2 cups fresh raspberries
½ cup sugar
¼ cup shortening
½ cup sugar
1 egg, well beaten
1 cup flour
1 tsp. baking powder
⅛ tsp. salt
¼ cup milk
½ tsp. vanilla

Place raspberries in bottom of greased 8" × 8" glass dish. Sprinkle ½ cup sugar over berries.

In bowl, cream shortening and ½ cup sugar and mix well. Add egg and mix again.

Sift flour, baking powder and salt and add to creamed shortening mixture. Blend in milk and vanilla and beat until smooth.

Drop batter by spoonfuls over top of fruit and bake at 350°F for 35 minutes.

This old fashioned cobbler is best served with lemon sauce (p.147).

Mrs. Moser's Apple Dumplings

An old fashioned dessert that kids love.

Syrup:

> 2 cups sugar
> 1 tsp. cinnamon
> ¼ tsp. nutmeg
> 2 cups water
> 2 tbsp. butter

Mix together ingredients in a medium-sized saucepan. Bring to a boil and then simmer for 5 minutes. Keep warm.

Dough:

> 2½ cups flour, sifted
> 4 tsp. baking powder
> ¾ tsp. salt
> ½ cup Crisco shortening
> ¾ cup milk, scant

Sift flour, baking powder, and salt into a bowl. Cut in shortening until crumbly. Stir in just enough milk to make a soft dough. Turn onto a floured board and knead lightly. Roll out to ¼ inch thickness and cut into 6 squares.

Apples: Pare, core, and slice 6 apples. Set aside sugar, cinnamon and butter for assembling.

Assemble: Put mound of apple slices in center of each square. Add a tbsp. of sugar, dash of cinnamon, and a dab of butter to each mound. Bring up the four corners of the pastry square and pinch all edges together to seal.

Place sealed side down in a greased 9″ × 13″ glass baking dish. Pour hot syrup over dumplings and then slit the top of each dumpling.

Bake at 425°F for 10 minutes. Lower heat to 375°F and bake 30-35 minutes longer.

Serve warm in their own syrup with plenty of cream.

Serves 6.

Pat's Apple Tart Dessert

Crust:

>½ cup butter
>⅓ cup sugar
>¼ tsp. vanilla
>1 cup flour

Filling:

>8 oz. cream cheese, softened
>¼ cup sugar
>1 egg, beaten
>½ tsp. vanilla

Topping:

>4 cups firm apples, peeled and sliced (¼" uniform slices)
>⅓ cup sugar
>¾ tsp. cinnamon
>½ cup almonds, sliced and toasted

Crust: Cream butter, add sugar, vanilla, and flour. Mix until smooth. Press into a 8" springform pan.

Filling: Combine ingredients and pour over crust.

Topping: Combine apples with sugar and cinnamon and toss gently so that apples do not break. Arrange on top of cream cheese mixture. Sprinkle with almonds.

Bake at 450°F for 10 minutes, lower heat to 400°F and bake for 25 minutes longer.

Serves 6-8.

Amaretto Cheesecake

Crust:

2 cups graham wafer crumbs
¼ cup sugar
⅓ cup butter, melted

Filling:

1½ lbs. cream cheese, softened
¾ cup sugar
4 eggs
1½ tsp. almond extract
¼ cup amaretto

Topping:

1 cup sour cream
2 tbsp. sugar
½ tsp. almond extract
1 tbsp. amaretto

½ cup sliced almonds, toasted

Crust: Mix together all ingredients and press into a 9″ springform pan.
Bake at 350°F for 5 minutes. Cool.

Filling: Beat cream cheese and sugar together until well blended. Beat in eggs, one at a time, until mixture is light and fluffy. Add flavourings and beat again. Pour into prepared crust and bake at 350°F for 40 to 45 minutes or until firm to touch.

Topping: While cake is baking, mix together topping ingredients. When cake is done, remove from oven and spoon on topping. Bake an additional 5-10 minutes. Remove from oven and sprinkle with toasted almonds. Let stand until well cooled. Refrigerate 8 hours or overnight before serving.

Serves 10-12.

 # Chocolate Kahlua
Cheesecake

Crust:

2 cups chocolate wafer crumbs
2 tbsp. sugar
¼ cup butter, melted

Filling:

1½ lb. cream cheese, softened
¾ cup sugar
3 eggs
¼ cup Kahlua
⅛ cup very strong coffee
5 oz. semi-sweet chocolate, melted

Topping:

1 cup sour cream
2 tbsp. sugar
1 tsp. vanilla or Kahlua

shaved chocolate

Crust: Mix together all ingredients and press into a 9″ springform pan. Bake at 350°F for 5 minutes. Cool.

Filling: Beat cream cheese and sugar together until well blended. Beat in eggs, one at a time, until mixture is light and fluffy. Add Kahlua, coffee and melted chocolate and beat until smooth.

Pour into prepared crust and bake at 350°F for 35 - 45 minutes or until firm to touch.

Topping: While cake is baking, mix together topping ingredients. When cake is done, remove from oven and spoon on topping. Bake an additional 5 to 10 minutes. Remove from oven and garnish with shaved chocolate. Let stand until well cooled. Refrigerate 8 hours or overnight before serving.

Serves 8-10.

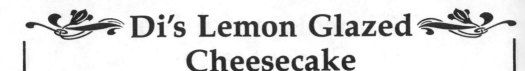

Di's Lemon Glazed Cheesecake

See picture pg. 112

Crust:

>2 cups graham wafer crumbs
>¼ cup sugar
>⅓ cup butter, melted

Filling:

>1½ lbs. cream cheese, softened
>¾ cup sugar
>3 eggs
>¼ cup lemon juice
>2 tsp. vanilla
>2 tsp. lemon peel, grated

Topping:

>2 cups sour cream
>3 tbsp. sugar
>1 tsp. vanilla

Lemon Glaze:

>½ cup sugar
>1½ tbsp. corn starch
>¼ tsp. salt
>¾ cup water
>⅓ cup lemon juice
>1 tsp. lemon rind, grated
>1 egg yolk, beaten
>1 tbsp. butter

Crust: Mix together all ingredients and press into a 9″ springform pan and bake at 350°F for 5 minutes. Cool.

Filling: Beat cream cheese and sugar together until well blended. Beat in eggs, one at a time, until mixture is light and fluffy. Add rest of ingredients and beat until smooth.

Pour into prepared crust and bake at 350°F for 35 minutes or until firm to touch.

Topping: While cake is baking, mix together topping ingredients. When cake is done, remove from oven and spoon on topping. Bake an additional 5 to 10 minutes. Remove from oven and cool for 1 hour and top with lemon glaze.

Lemon Glaze: Mix sugar, corn starch and salt together in small sauce pan. Add rest of ingredients except butter and stir over medium heat until mixture is thickened. Add butter. Cool slightly. Pour over cake and refrigerate cake for 6 hours or overnight.

Lindy's Cheesecake

Shortbread Crust:

>2 cups flour
>½ cup sugar
>2 tsp. lemon rind, grated
>1 tsp. vanilla
>¾ cup butter, softened
>1 tsp. lemon juice
>1 egg yolk

Filling:

>2½ lbs. cream cheese, softened
>1½ cups sugar
>3 tbsp. flour
>2 tsp. lemon rind
>1½ tsp. orange rind
>¼ tsp. vanilla
>5 eggs
>¼ cup whipping cream

Fruit Topping:

>1 pkg. sweet frozen sliced strawberries, thawed
>¼ cup cold water
>2 tbsp. cornstarch

Crust: Put all ingredients in a food processor and process until well blended.

Press into bottom and up sides of a 10" springform pan.

Bake at 400°F for 6 to 7 minutes.

Filling: Cream together cream cheese and sugar until smooth. Add rest of ingredients except cream and blend well. Stir in cream and pour into prepared crust.

Bake at 450°F for 10 minutes, reduce heat to 300°F and bake for an additional 45 minutes or until firm to touch. Turn off oven, open door slightly and leave cake to cool.

Refrigerate overnight and top with fruit topping.

Fruit Topping: Place strawberries in saucepan. Add cornstarch to cold water and mix well. Add to strawberries. Cook over medium heat, stirring frequently unitl thickened. Cool.

New York Cheesecake

An original New York cheesecake!

Crust:

2 cups graham wafer crumbs
¼ cup sugar
⅓ cup butter, melted
dash cinnamon or nutmeg (optional)

Filling:

2 lbs. cream cheese, softened
¾ cup sugar
2 large eggs
1 tsp. vanilla
2 tbsp. cornstarch
1 cup sour cream

Topping:

2 cups sour cream
2 tbsp. sugar
1 tsp. vanilla

Crust: Mix together all ingredients and press into a 9″ springform pan and bake at 350°F for 5 minutes. Cool.

Filling: Beat cream cheese and sugar together until well blended. Beat in eggs, one at a time until mixture is light and fluffy. Add vanilla, corn starch and sour cream and blend well. Pour into prepared crust and bake at 350°F for 45 minutes or until firm to touch.

Topping: While cake is baking, mix together topping ingredients. When cake is done, remove from oven and spoon on topping. Bake an additional 5 to 10 minutes. Remove from oven and let stand for 1 hour. Refrigerate overnight before serving.

Serves 10-12.

 # Pumpkin Walnut Cheesecake

This was our cheesecake company's most popular recipe, here it is —

Crust:

> 1½ cups graham wafer crumbs
> ¼ cup sugar
> ¼ cup walnuts, crushed
> ⅓-½ cups butter, melted

Filling:

> 1½ lbs. cream cheese, softened
> ¾ cup brown sugar, packed
> ¾ cup granulated sugar
> 5 eggs
> 1 - 14 oz. can pumpkin
> 1¾ tsp. pumpkin pie spice
> ¼ cup whipping cream

Topping:

> 6 tbsp. butter, melted
> 1 cup brown sugar, firmly packed
> 1 cup walnuts, coarsely chopped
>
> whip cream for garnish

Crust: Mix together all ingredients and press into bottom and slightly up the sides of a lightly greased 10" springform pan.

Bake at 350°F for 5 minutes. Cool.

Filling: In a large mixing bowl, beat cream cheese and sugars together until well blended. Beat in eggs, one at a time, until mixture is light and fluffy. Add pumpkin and spice and mix well. Beat in whipping cream at low speed until smooth. Pour into prepared crust and bake at 325°F for 1 hour and 35 minutes or until firm to touch.

Topping: Combine melted butter, brown sugar and nuts and mix until crumbly. When cake is done, remove from oven and sprinkle with walnut topping and bake an additional 10 minutes.

Cool and refrigerate for at least 6 hours or overnight.

Garnish with whipping cream.

Serves 10-12.

Chocolate
Grand Marnier Mousse

Easy and elegant — make in a blender.
More like a pudding — no egg whites.

1¼ cups whipping cream
8 oz. semi-sweet chocolate chips
⅓ cup sugar
5 large egg yolks
1 tbsp. Grand Marnier
1½ tsp. orange peel, grated
1½ tsp. vanilla
4 tbsp. butter, room temperature

In a small saucepan, heat cream over medium heat until tiny bubbles appear around the edge.

Put chocolate chips, sugar, yolks, liqueur, orange peel and vanilla in blender or food processor. Pour in hot cream and blend one minute on high speed. Drop in butter one tablespoon at a time, process after each addition. Pour mousse into serving dish. Cover and refrigerate at least 3 hours.

Serves 6.

Photo: Aunt Glady's Butter Tarts, page 138.

Shelagh's
Chocolate Bombe

Makes 2 desserts: 1 serves 8-10 and the other serves at least 6.
Make ahead and freeze up to 3 months.

1 angelfood cake mix
1 cup semi-sweet chocolate chips
8 oz. soft cream cheese
¾ cup maple syrup
1 tsp. instant coffee
1 cup whipping cream

Per Cake:

¼ cup coffee liqueur
2 cups whipping cream
1-2 tbsp. sugar
shaved chocolate

Prepare angelfood cake mix as per directions on package. Bake in 2 ungreased ovenproof bowls, (2½ qt. and a 4 cup). Bake for 30 minutes.

When cool remove from bowls. Scoop out centre, leaving a 2" thick shell. Return shell to clean bowls.

Melt chocolate chips over hot water.

Beat cream cheese at medium speed until light and fluffy. Slowly beat in maple syrup and instant coffee.

Fold chocolate into cheese mixture. Beat 1 cup of whipping cream until stiff. Fold into cheese mixture and pour into cake shells. Cover with plastic wrap and freeze.

About 2 hours before serving - remove bombe(s) from freezer. Invert onto a serving plate. Drizzle surface with ¼ cup coffee liqueur.

Beat 2 cups (per bombe) whipping cream with sugar and frost bombe. Garnish with shaved chocolate.

Regrigerate.

 # Chocolate Mousse Pie

This delicious pie can be prepared ahead and frozen.

Crust:

2½ cups chocolate wafer crumbs
¼ cup sugar
2 tsp. cinnamon
½ cup butter, melted

Filling:

16 oz. semi-sweet chocolate
½ cup butter
2 cups icing sugar
6 egg yolks
2 cups whipping cream
1 tbsp. vanilla or rum
6 egg whites

Garnish:

2 cups whipped cream
sugar
shaved chocolate

Crust: Mix together crumbs, sugar, cinnamon and butter. Press into bottom and half way up the sides of a 10″ springform pan. Refrigerate. Refrigerate.

Filling: In top of double boiler, melt chocolate and butter.

In bowl, beat icing sugar, egg yolks, melted chocolate and butter.

Whip cream with vanilla.

In another bowl, beat egg whites until stiff peaks form.

Add whipped cream to chocolate mixture alternately with beaten egg whites.

Pour mousse into prepared crust and refrigerate.

To serve decorate with whipped cream and shaved chocolate.

Serves 10-12.

 # Cold Zabaglione

4 egg yolks
½ cup sugar
¼ cup Amaretto liqueur
½ cup dry white wine
1½ cups whipping cream
2 oz. almonds, slivered and toasted

In top of a double boiler, add sugar to egg yolks and beat with a whisk until frothy. Place over low heat, adding Amaretto and wine. Beat with electric beater until thick. Remove from heat and cool.

Whip cream and fold into cooled mixture. Pour into stemmed glasses and sprinkle with almonds. Refrigerate.

Serve with sugar cookies.

Fudge-Coffee Ice-Cream Squares

2½ cups vanilla wafer crumbs
3 oz. unsweetened chocolate
¼ lb. butter
2 cups icing sugar
4 eggs, separated
1½ cups pecan halves
2 litres coffee ice-cream

shaved chocolate for garnish

Sprinkle 1¾ cups crumbs over bottom of a 9″ × 13″ greased dish.

In a medium saucepan melt chocolate and butter over low heat. Remove from heat. Stir in icing sugar.

Beat egg yolks and stir into chocolate mixture.

Beat egg whites until stiff and fold into chocolate mixture, blending well. Pour mixture over crumbs. Top with pecans and freeze until solid.

Soften ice-cream, spread it over chocolate layer and top with remaining crumbs and garnish with chocolate. Cover with foil and freeze until solid.

Cut into 2½″ squares.

Serves 16-20.

Hazelnut
Chocolate Bar Dessert

Crust:

2 cups chocolate wafer crumbs
2 tbsp. sugar
¼ cup butter, melted

Filling:

½ cup milk
18 marshmallows
3 or 4 - 100 grams hazelnut chocolate bars
2 cups whipping cream
2 tbsp. rum

whipped cream
sugar
shaved chocolate

Crust: Mix together crumbs, sugar, and melted butter. Press into a 9" × 13" buttered glass dish. Refrigerate.

Filling: Heat milk in a double boiler, add marshmallows and chocolate bars and stir until melted. Set aside.

Whip cream with rum until soft peaks form and fold into hazelnut mixture. Pour into prepared dish. Decorate with whipped cream and shaved chocolate and refrigerate.

Serves 8-10.

 # Sheila's Ice-Cream
Bombe

Make this a day ahead.

3-3½ cups vanilla ice-cream, slightly softened
2 squares unsweetened chocolate
¼ cup water
½ cup sugar
⅛ tsp. salt
2 egg yolks, slightly beaten
1 tsp. vanilla
1 tsp. rum
1 cup whipping cream
½ cup raisins, finely chopped
½ cup figs, finely chopped

Line a 1½ qt. mold with ice-cream and freeze until firm — about 1 hour.

Combine chocolate and water, melting over very low heat and stir constantly until blended. Mix in sugar and salt and simmer for 3 minutes, stirring constantly.

Gradually pour hot chocolate mixture over beaten egg yolks, blending well. Cool and add vanilla and rum.

Beat whipping cream until stiff, fold into the chocolate mixture along with the raisins and figs. Spoon mixture into centre of mold. Return to freezer and freeze overnight. Unmold for serving.

A nice change from the traditional Christmas pudding.
Serves 8.

Pink Lemonade Pie

A summertime dessert.

Crust:

> 1¼ cups graham wafer crumbs
> ⅓ cup brown sugar, packed
> 2 tbsp. flour
> ⅓ cup butter, melted

Filling:

> 1 - 8 oz. pkg. cream cheese, softened
> 1 - 11 oz. can sweetened condensed milk
> 1 - 6 oz. can frozen pink lemonade concentrate, thawed
> 3 drops red food colouring
> 1 cup whipping cream

Crust: Combine crumbs, sugar, flour and butter in a medium bowl. Press into bottom and up sides of a 9" pie plate. Chill.

Filling: In a large bowl, beat cream cheese until fluffy. Gradually beat in sweetened milk, lemonade and food colouring.

In a chilled bowl, beat cream until stiff peaks form. Fold whipped cream into lemonade mixture and chill 30 minutes. Pour into crust and freeze until firm (at least 6 hours).

Remove from freezer 10-20 minutes before serving.

Lemon Ice

This will surprise you — it is so easy to make and tastes so good!

> 1 cup milk
> 1 cup whipping cream
> 1 cup sugar
> juice of 2 lemons
> grated rind of 1 lemon

In a bowl mix milk, cream and sugar together and stir until sugar is dissolved. Freeze for approximately 2 hours or until crystals form.

Remove from freezer. Add lemon juice and rind and beat all together. Pour into serving bowl and freeze.

Variation: Reduce sugar and serve small scoops topped with champagne as a palate cleanser.

Lemon Souffle
with Grand Marnier Sauce

An elegant ending to a dinner party.

> 5 egg yolks
> 1½ cups sugar
> juice of 3 lemons (½ cup)
> rind of one lemon, grated
> 2 pkgs. gelatin
> ½ cup water
> 2 cups whipping cream
> 5 egg whites

Beat yolks and sugar together. Gradually add lemon juice and rind and beat until thick. In a saucepan, soak gelatin in water until soft and dissolve over low heat. Do not boil. Remove from heat and set aside.

Whip cream lightly and add to lemon egg mixture. Add cooked gelatin to this and stir until mixture begins to thicken.

Beat egg whites until stiff. Fold into lemon mixture.

Pour mixture into glass serving bowl and refrigerate for several hours or until set.

Serve with Grand Marnier Sauce (p.145).

Serves 10-12.

Overnight
Meringue

Make this quick meringue the night before and fill it with your favourite topping.

> 6 egg whites, at room temperature
> ¼ tsp. salt
> ½ tsp. cream of tartar
> 1½ cups sugar
> 1 tsp. vanilla
> ¼ cup light rum (optional)

Toppings:

> a. 1½ cups whipped cream
> 2-3 tbsp. sugar
> 1 tsp. vanilla
> 2 cups fresh berries

> or

> b. chocolate sauce (p.144)
> 1½ cups whipped cream
> 2-3 tbsp. sugar
> 1 tsp. vanilla

Preheat oven to 450°F.

The day before serving, in large bowl of electric mixer, mix together egg whites, salt and cream of tartar and beat until frothy. At high speed, beat in sugar gradually, beating well after each addition. Add vanilla and beat until stiff peaks form. Turn into lightly buttered 10" springform pan. Place on middle rack of oven, turn off oven and let stand overnight (do not peek).

In the morning, loosen edges and turn out onto serving plate. Sprinkle with rum if desired and refrigerate.

When ready to serve, top with berries and whipped cream or chocolate sauce with whipped cream.

Nathan's Pastry

Never fails.

> 5 cups flour
> 1 tsp. salt
> 2 tsp. baking powder
> 1 lb. Tenderflake lard
> 2 tsp. white vinegar
> 1 egg — slightly beaten add water to vinegar and egg to make 1 cup

Mix together flour, salt and baking powder. Cut in lard until crumbly. Add liquid and mix gently with hands. Roll into a ball. Roll out amount needed on a floured board.

Refrigerate or freeze remainder.

Makes 3 - 2 crust pies or 3½ dozen tart shells — muffin size.

Aunt Gladys'
Butter Tarts

These large tarts are truly indigenous to Canada. Be careful! After one bite, hot from the oven with the buttery sauce dribbling down your chin, you'll be addicted!

See picture opposite page 128.

1 recipe Nathan's pastry (p.137)

2 cups brown sugar
2 cups corn syrup
½ lb. butter, not margarine
8 eggs
½ tsp. salt
1½ tsp. vanilla
3 cups dark raisins

Roll out pastry to ⅛ inch thickness and line muffin tins. Set aside.

In large saucepan mix together brown sugar and syrup and bring to a boil. Boil for 5 minutes. Add butter to mixture and stir until melted.

Slightly beat the eggs in a large bowl and gradually add the hot mixture, beating constantly. Add salt and vanilla and mix well.

Place 1 heaping tablespoon of raisins into each tart shell and pour in the hot mixture almost to the top of the shells.

Bake at 400°F for 15 to 20 minutes or until pastry is golden brown. Remove from oven and cool before removing from tins.

Makes 24 large tarts. Freeze well.

 # Fresh Berry Pie

An unbaked berry pie

1 - 9 inch baked pie shell

4 cups fresh berries
2½ tbsp. cornstarch
¾ cup sugar
⅔ cup water
1 tbsp. lemon juice
2 tbsp. butter

whipped cream for garnish

Mix 1 cup of the berries with cornstarch, sugar and water. Cook over medium heat, stirring gently until thickened. Remove from heat, stir in lemon juice and butter. Chill in refrigerator for ½ to ¾ hour.

Fold in remainder of berries and pour into baked pastry shell. Refrigerate for several hours or until set.

Serve with whipped cream.

Lemon Angel
Meringue Tart

Make the meringue pie shell the night before.

Meringue Tart:

> 4 egg whites, at room temperature
> ¼ tsp. cream of tartar
> ¼ tsp. salt
> ¾ cup sugar

Topping:

> 4 egg yolks
> 1 tbsp. lemon rind, grated
> 3 tbsp. lemon juice
> ½ cup sugar
> dash of salt
> 1 tbsp. butter

Garnish:

> 1 cup whipped cream
> fresh strawberries

Preheat oven to 450°F.

The day before serving, in a large bowl of electric mixer, mix together egg whites, cream of tartar and salt and beat until frothy. At high speed, beat in sugar gradually, beating well after each addition. Beat until stiff peaks form. Turn into lightly buttered 9" pie plate. Place on middle rack of oven, turn off oven and let stand overnight (do not peek.)

In top of a double boiler, over boiling water, beat egg yolks until thick and lemon coloured. Gradually beat in peel, juice, sugar and salt. Cook until thickened, stirring constantly (7 to 8 minutes). Stir in butter. Cover and cool.

Spread half the whipped cream in prepared pie shell. Spoon on lemon filling, then add remaining whipped cream. Chill for at least 4 hours.

Garnish with strawberries.

Pear Pie

An easy fall dessert — no paring, just cut pears in half and core!

1 - 9″ unbaked pie shell

3-4 Bartlett pears
1 cup sugar
¼ cup flour
¼ cup butter
2 eggs
1 tsp. vanilla

Cut pears in half lengthwise. Remove cores and arrange pears cut side down in shell in a circular fashion.

Beat remaining ingredients until smooth and pour over pears.

Bake at 325°F for 40-45 minutes.

 # Raspberry Pie

pastry for 2 crust 9" pie.
see Nathan's pastry (p.137)

4 cups raspberries (loganberries or blackberries)
1 cup sugar
¼ cup flour
¼ cup butter, cut into small pieces

sugar

Line a 9" pie plate with pastry.
Gently mix raspberries with sugar and flour. Pour berries into shell, dot with butter. Place top crust on pie and score. Sprinkle with sugar.
Bake at 400°F for 10 minutes, turn oven down to 350°F and continue baking for 25 minutes or until pie is golden brown and bubbling.

Note: To ensure edges do not burn, shape narrow pieces of tin foil around outside edges of crust.

Rhubarb Custard Pie

pastry for 2 crust 9" pie
see Nathan's pastry (p.137)

1½ cups sugar
¼ cup flour
¼ tsp. nutmeg
dash of salt
3 eggs, well beaten
4 cups rhubarb, cut into 1 inch slices

2 tbsp. butter
sugar

Line a 9" inch pie plate with pastry. Mix sugar, flour, nutmeg, and salt. Add dry ingredients to beaten eggs. Mix well. Stir in rhubarb.
Fill pie shell with rhubarb mixture. Dot with butter and top with crust. Score top crust and sprinkle with sugar.
Bake at 400°F for 50 minutes.
Watch edges of crust and cover with strips of tin foil if becoming too brown.

Sauces

Chocolate Sauce #1

Quick and easy.

> ½ cup sugar
> 1 tbsp. cornstarch
> 2 tbsp cocoa powder
> 1 cup water
> 1 tbsp butter
> ½ tsp. vanilla

In a small saucepan mix sugar, cornstarch, and cocoa. Add water and bring to a boil. Add the butter and vanilla and mix well.
Serve hot over ice cream.
Store in refrigerator.

Chocolate Sauce #2

Make this ahead, refrigerate and then reheat.

> 1 cup butter
> 2 squares semi-sweet chocolate
> 1½ cups sugar
> ½ cup cocoa powder
> 1 cup whipping cream
> 2 tsp. vanilla

Melt butter and chocolate over low heat. Add sugar, cocoa and cream. Bring to a boil and add vanilla. Remove from heat and blend well.

 # Grand Marnier
Sauce

Serve this over lemon souffle (p.135) for a really spectacular tasting dessert.

½ cup whipping cream
3 egg yolks
¼ cup sugar
⅓ cup butter, melted and cooled
3 tbsp. lemon juice
1 tsp. lemon peel, grated
3 tbsp. Grand Marnier

Beat cream until thick and glossy, but not stiff. Refrigerate.
Beat yolks until thick and lemon coloured and gradually add sugar. Slowly beat in cooled, melted butter, lemon juice, peel and liqueur. Fold in whipped cream. Chill well.

 # Hazelnut Praline
Sauce

Make the praline in advance ready to be mixed with whipped cream for a delicious topping for fresh fruit.

½ cup sugar
⅓ cup whole hazelnuts

1 cup whipping cream
2 egg yolks
1 cup icing sugar
1 tsp. vanilla

In a heavy skillet, combine sugar and hazelnuts and cook over medium heat, stirring frequently until sugar is melted and deep brown. Pour praline into a buttered shallow pan and set aside until it hardens. Remove from pan, break into pieces and put into blender until chunky. (At this point, the praline can be kept in a glass jar in your cupboard, do not refrigerate).

Whip cream until it holds its shape. Beat egg yolks with icing sugar and vanilla until mixture is smooth and thick. Fold into whipped cream and add praline. Spoon sauce immediately over fruit.

We like to make a layered fruit salad in a glass bowl and serve this sauce over it.

 # Lemon Sauce

For fruit cobblers see Raspberry Cobbler (p.119)

½ cup sugar
1 tbsp. cornstarch
dash of salt
1 cup boiling water
1 egg yolk, slightly beaten
3 tbsp. lemon juice
2 tbsp. butter

Mix sugar, cornstarch and salt in a saucepan. Add boiling water and cook gently for 15 minutes, stirring often. Remove from heat and add egg yolk, lemon juice and butter. Mix well and serve warm.

Olive's Rum Sauce

A must with plum pudding!

¾ cup brown sugar
1 tbsp. cornstarch
pinch of salt
1 cup boiling water
1 tbsp. butter
½ tsp. vanilla
¼-⅓ cup rum

Mix sugar, cornstarch and salt in a medium saucepan. Add boiling water slowly and cook over medium-high heat until slightly thickened and there is no taste of cornstarch. Add butter and vanilla.
To serve add rum and mix well.

This sauce is so good that you will want lots — this recipe doubles or triples easily!

4 servings.

Mrs. Tye's Barbecue Sauce

This makes a large amount of sauce that we keep in our refrigerator for easy barbecuing.

2 - 14 oz. bottles ketchup
2 - 10 oz. bottles chili sauce
⅓ cup prepared mustard
1 tbsp. dry mustard
1½ cups brown sugar, packed
2 tbsp. coarse pepper
1½ cups wine vinegar
1 cup lemon juice
½ cup HP sauce
¼ cup Worcestershire sauce
Tabasco, few dashes
1 tbsp. soy sauce
2 tbsp. salad oil
1 bottle of beer

Combine all ingredients. Store in refrigerator in glass jar ready for your next barbecue. Keeps indefinitely.

Basting Sauce
for Pork

Use as a baste for ham or pork roast.

¼ cup brown sugar
2 tbsp. lemon juice
2 tbsp. oil
2 tbsp. honey
1 tsp. allspice
1 tsp. cinnamon

In a small saucepan combine all ingredients and bring to a boil. Baste ham or pork the last half hour of cooking.

Cranberry Sauce

Make this zesty sauce while the turkey is roasting — you won't regret it.

½ cup water
½ cup orange juice
1 cup sugar
1 lb. whole cranberries
2 tbsp. orange rind, grated

In a saucepan, mix water, juice and sugar together. Heat until sugar is dissolved. Add cranberries, bring to a boil and cook for 3 to 5 minutes, stirring occasionally until berries are soft. Do not overcook. Remove from heat, stir in orange rind. Cool and chill for 2 hours before serving.

 # Plum Sauce

Serve this with sesame chicken pieces (p.12).

      1 - 12 oz. jar plum jam
      2 tbsp. vinegar
      1 tbsp. brown sugar, packed
      1 tbsp. green onion, finely chopped
      1 tsp. dried, finely chopped red chili pepper
      1 clove garlic, minced
      ½ tsp. ground ginger

Combine all ingredients in a small saucepan and bring to a boil, stirring constantly. Remove from heat and cool.
Refrigerate in covered container.
Serve hot or cold.

INDEX